Pronunciation Pedagogy and Theory
New Views, New Directions

Pronunciation Pedagogy and Theory: New Views, New Directions

Joan Morley
Editor

Teachers of English to Speakers of Other Languages, Inc.

Typeset in Caledonia by
World Composition Services, Inc., Sterling, Virginia
and printed by
Pantagraph Printing, Bloomington, Illinois USA

Copyright © 1994 by Teachers of English to Speakers of Other Languages, Inc.
(TESOL).

All rights reserved. Copying or further publication of the contents of this work is
not permitted without permission of TESOL, except for limited "fair use" for
educational, scholarly, and similar purposes as authorized by U.S. Copyright Law,
in which case appropriate notice of the source of the work should be given.

Helen Kornblum *Director of Communications and Marketing*
Ellen Garshick *Copy Editor*
Ann Kammerer *Cover*

Teachers of English to Speakers of Other Languages, Inc.
1600 Cameron Street, Suite 300
Alexandria, VA 22314 USA
Tel 703-836-0774 • Fax 703-836-7864

ISBN 939791-55-2
Library of Congress Catalog No. 94-060896

Contents

Contributors	xii
Introduction	1
1. Pronunciation Assessment in the ESL/EFL Curriculum *Janet Goodwin, Donna Brinton, and Marianne Celce-Murcia*	3
2. Empowering Students With Predictive Skills *Wayne B. Dickerson*	17
3. Intonation: A Navigation Guide for the Listener *Judy B. Gilbert*	36
4. Some Perspectives on Accent: Range of Voice Quality Variation, the Periphery, and Focusing *John H. Esling*	49
5. A Multidimensional Curriculum Design for Speech-Pronunciation Instruction *Joan Morley*	64
6. Recent Research in L2 Phonology: Implications for Practice *Martha C. Pennington*	92
7. The Effects of Pronunciation Teaching *George Yule and Doris Macdonald*	109

Contributors

Donna Brinton
University of California, Los Angeles

Marianne Celce-Murcia
University of California, Los Angeles

Wayne B. Dickerson
University of Illinois at Urbana-Champaign

John H. Esling
University of Victoria

Judy B. Gilbert
University of California, Berkeley Extension

Janet Goodwin
University of California, Los Angeles

Doris Macdonald
Northern Illinois University

Joan Morley
The University of Michigan

Martha C. Pennington
City Polytechnic of Hong Kong

George Yule
Louisiana State University

Introduction

One sign of the times in the field of ESL over the past 15 years has been a reawakening of concern for and interest in verbal language—including pronunciation. But pronunciation course work today, though it carries the same name, has been expanded and altered in many programs. Perhaps *communicative pronunciation* more clearly reflects the current view that pronunciation in the L2 curriculum is an *integral part of communication*, not a drill-based exercise component set aside from the mainstream of instruction. The renewal of interest has flourished as innovative specialists in curricular design and materials development for pronunciation have explored some new and fruitful directions in the principles and practices of teaching pronunciation.

Clearly, since TESOL's publication of the first theme volume on pronunciation (J. Morley, Ed., 1987, *Current Perspectives on Pronunciation: Practices Anchored in Theory*), many facets of pronunciation endeavor have grown steadily. In contrast to the handful of pronunciation-focused papers published in the 1970s, throughout the 1980s and into the 1990s the number of journal articles, teacher resource books, and student texts available has continued to increase. At the same time professional presentations on pronunciation, in the form of more and more conference papers, workshops, demonstrations, and colloquia at local, national, and international conferences, have increased significantly.

Overall, educators today seem to be renewing their professional commitment to empowering students to become effective, fully participating members of the English-speaking community in which they "communicate." One part of this movement is a persistent effort to write pronunciation back into the instructional equation but with a new look and a basic premise: *Intelligible pronunciation is an essential component of communicative competence.*

This volume contains expanded versions of seven papers presented in 1992 at the 26th Annual TESOL Convention in Vancouver, BC. The papers discuss a range of topics in pedagogy, theory, and research that cut across a broad spectrum of important issues in today's "new-look" pronunciation picture.

The first paper, by Janet Goodwin, Donna Brinton, and Marianne Celce-

Murcia, focuses on pronunciation assessment: diagnostic evaluation, ongoing evaluation with feedback, and classroom achievement testing procedures. In the second paper Wayne B. Dickerson makes a strong case for guiding students in setting goals for spelling-pronunciation empowerment and suggests a variety of rules teachers can use in developing a program. Next Judy B. Gilbert highlights the importance of intonation instruction in today's pronunciation curriculum. Her practical classroom suggestions for teachers focus on topics that must be taught and methods for teaching them. John H. Esling explores quite a different area, calling attention to two levels of speech analysis—the narrower, short-term segmental dimension and the broader voice quality settings dimension (also termed *long-term articulatory postures*)—and describes in detail voice quality variations and research on voice quality settings in social contexts, together with implications for ESL instruction. In the fifth paper Joan Morley presents a multidimensional curriculum design for speech-pronunciation instruction and a variety of features to consider. Martha Pennington clearly and concisely reviews the research in six major areas of L2 phonology and its implications for practice. Finally, George Yule and Doris Macdonald present findings from their research study on the effects of pronunciation teaching, focusing on the study of learner pronunciation patterns as a result of specific instructional procedures.

Taken together, these papers constitute an important resource for teacher trainees, novice instructors, and experienced teachers.

— 1 —
Pronunciation Assessment in the ESL/EFL Curriculum

Janet Goodwin, Donna Brinton, and Marianne Celce-Murcia
University of California, Los Angeles

Editorial Notes

Pronunciation has recently taken its rightful place as an essential component of ESL/EFL instruction. But as Janet Goodwin, Donna Brinton, and Marianne Celce-Murcia observe, most work on pronunciation has dealt with content, teaching strategies, and materials rather than with assessment. The purpose of their paper is to discuss and make suggestions on three types of pronunciation assessment: diagnostic evaluation, ongoing evaluation with feedback, and classroom achievement testing procedures. They also describe in an appendix some of the formal oral proficiency examinations that include assessment of the pronunciation skill in their battery of tests.

The authors first discuss features of the *diagnostic evaluation of pronunciation*, a process that yields a global assessment of the learner's comprehensibility. Diagnostic assessment can help to determine the learner's proficiency level in pronunciation and to analyze individual learners' needs; the information can then serve as a basis for making an appropriate instructional placement and planning a syllabus. One aspect of diagnostic assessment, *perception*, provides information about the learner's ability to process features of the English sound system. The authors give examples of test items that assess perceptual abilities in the following areas: consonant-vowel discrimination, word stress, sentence stress and intonation, and reduced speech. As for the other aspect of diagnostic assessment, *production*, Goodwin, Brinton, and Celce-Murcia suggest that teachers obtain two types of speech samples from learners. For the first, taken as learners read a standardized script, it is important to write or select a reading passage that incorporates as many features of English pronunciation as possible, in context, to assure the inclusion of pronunciation features that might not occur naturally in a spontaneous speech sample. For the second speech sample, free speech, teachers should take care to obtain a sample of sustained speech (i.e., an open-ended sample of impromptu speaking), not just answers to simple questions.

The authors next take up the topic of *ongoing evaluation with feedback*, which encompasses ongoing learner assessment and error correction. This type of assessment enables the teacher to evaluate student progress and provides a mechanism for giving learners continuous informal feedback. Three types of techniques—self-correction, peer feedback, and teacher correction—are discussed along with examples of activities and evaluation procedures in all three areas.

The section on *classroom achievement testing* focuses on tests administered to determine the learner's level of achievement on specific, course-related measures. These tests, though similar in design to diagnostic tests, are based on the precise material that has been taught and measure students' progress within the framework of one particular course and curriculum (in contrast to diagnostic tests, which focus on the learner's overall command of English pronunciation). Tests for both perception and production are discussed.

Finally, the authors briefly discuss formal oral proficiency testing instruments, observing that although many commercial proficiency tests ignore pronunciation skills, a number assess pronunciation either as a discrete entity or as one component in the overall oral proficiency profile.

The authors stress that ESL/EFL teachers who work on pronunciation in the classroom must have a thorough knowledge of assessment tools and strategies and the ability to apply them appropriately in placing students, analyzing their needs, designing curriculum, giving feedback, and measuring achievement.

J.M.

Pronunciation Assessment in the ESL/EFL Curriculum

The teaching of pronunciation has at times been considered almost a luxury in the ESL/EFL curriculum, unlike reading, writing, listening, and general speaking fluency. But in recent years pronunciation has come to be recognized as an essential component in most ESL/EFL instructional programs. The issue of assessment, however, has been somewhat neglected in discussions of teaching pronunciation, which have focused primarily on content (phonetics), teaching strategies, and materials. Because pronunciation instruction often requires an individualized approach, teachers also need a solid grounding in three important areas of pronunciation assessment: diagnostic evaluation, ongoing evaluation with feedback, and classroom testing. In addition, teachers should be aware of formal oral proficiency instruments that include an assessment of pronunciation skills in their overall proficiency profile.

Diagnostic Evaluation

Like the evaluation of other skills, the diagnostic evaluation of learners' pronunciation, both perception and production, is a means of determining their proficiency level. It has both a screening or placement function and a needs analysis function. Regarding the former, the assessment procedures are generally used to place learners in courses or to assess whether a given individual has sufficient skill in pronunciation to perform a certain task (e.g., speaks intelligibly enough to serve as a graduate teaching assistant or a medical receptionist). Within the context of a specific course, the assessment procedures assist the teacher in analyzing the learners' needs. Performed at the outset of the course, they are the teacher's initial method of setting curricular objectives and focusing on the needs of a particular population of students. From diagnostic evaluation the teacher can gain valuable information about individual learners' difficulties and about which syllabus elements to emphasize. In sum, diagnostic evaluation of pronunciation is a global assessment of the learners' comprehensibility. How intelligible is the learn-

6   Pronunciation Pedagogy and Theory

ers' pronunciation? What kind of errors are they making? Teachers certainly need to diagnose the learners' *production*; equally crucial is an accurate diagnosis of the learners' *perception*, that is, how well they are able to process features of the English sound system.

Perception

Below are examples of formats to use in diagnosing learners' ability to discriminate consonant and vowel distinctions, word stress, sentence stress, intonation, and reduced speech patterns. The list does not include all features of English pronunciation; it serves as a basis upon which to evaluate learners' perception.[1]

Consonant-vowel discrimination. The teacher reads a sentence with one of the two choices in the minimal pair.[2] Students either

1. underline the word they hear:
   a. He (bit/beat) the man.
   b. He's gone to (back/pack) the car up.
2. or circle the picture that represents the sentence they hear:

   a.

   b.

Word stress.   Students mark the choice that shows the syllable receiving the main stress (capitals = main stress):

   (on tape) *Computer* games have become very *popular*.
   a. COMputer   a. POPular
   b comPUTer   b. poPUlar
   c. compuTER   c. popuLAR

(on tape) American children spend hours at this *activity.*
a. ACtivity
b. acTIVity
c. activiTY

Sentence stress. Students mark the choice that best represents the proper stress pattern (capitals = stress):

(on tape) Hi, I'm Mark Johnson. What's your name?
a. HI, I'm MARK Johnson. WHAT'S your name?
b. HI, I'M Mark JOHNson. What's YOUR name?
c. Hi, I'M Mark Johnson. What's your NAME?

(on tape) Patricia Smith, but you can call me Pat.
a. PaTRIcia Smith, BUT you can call ME Pat.
b. PATricia SMITH, but you CAN call me PAT.
c. PaTRIcia SMITH, but YOU can call me PAT.

Sentence stress and intonation. Students listen and choose the statement that best represents the meaning of the speaker:

(on tape) Can you make it to lunch on THURSday?
a. I know your sister can't, but can you?
b. OK, you can't make it for dinner, so how about lunch?
c. If you can't make it on Wednesday, how about Thursday?

Reduced speech. In the following dialog, one or more words are missing in each blank. Students listen to the two speakers and write the full form of the missing words in each blank:

(on tape)
A: What _____ do tomorrow?
       (1. are you going to)
B: I _____ . Do you _____ go to the beach?
   (2. don't know)   (3. want to)
A: Sounds great! _____ pick me up at 10?
                 (4. Can you)
B: No problem. _____ then.
               (5. See you)

Production

For more complete information on a student's pronunciation, a speech sample, preferably on tape, is also necessary. In general, it is best to obtain two sample types: a standardized sample of the learner reading aloud and a sample of the learner's spontaneous speech.

In the reading-aloud task, teachers can guide students to show their command of pronunciation features that might not naturally occur in a spontaneous speech sample. In addition, if the syllabus allows limited time for teaching pronunciation, teachers can use a comparative analysis of all students' speech patterns to determine features for the primary focus of the class instruction. One well-known standardized passage is the one offered by Prator and Robinett (1985). Although some published examples of diagnostic pronunciation tests consist of individual words or sentences, we believe a single passage incorporating many features is essential for contextualization. Because a reading-aloud test may not yield the most natural evidence of a speaker's pronunciation, a sample of spontaneous speech should also be elicited. The topic may be either open ended, such as talking about one's hometown, family, or hobbies, or more controlled, such as narrating a story sequence around a series of pictures or commenting on a cartoon strip.[3]

Having carried out a diagnostic evaluation of learners' perception and production, the teacher can address the most pressing pronunciation needs of the students within the time and curriculum of a specific course. The next step in pronunciation assessment involves continuous evaluation and feedback during each lesson.

Ongoing Evaluation With Feedback

Feedback includes both ongoing learner assessment and error correction. It not only is the domain of teachers but involves peer and self-correction as well. The purpose of such evaluation and feedback in the classroom is twofold. On the one hand, the teacher needs to evaluate students' progress in order to individualize instruction as much as possible and revise the curriculum if necessary. Furthermore, the teacher should give continuous informal feedback on individual progress so that each learner can improve during the period of instruction. The feedback may take the form of opportunities for self-correction, peer feedback, or teacher correction. The techniques below allow learners to discover their own errors and to correct themselves. Formats requiring a knowledge of phonetic symbols can be used only with students who have learned a phonetic alphabet.

Self-correction

The teacher can create opportunities for self-correction in the following ways:

1. by writing the utterance on the board and underlining the mispronounced feature:
   I haven't made a deci<u>sion</u>.

(The student had mispronounced the underlined sound /dž/ instead of /ž/.)
2. by writing the type of error on the board:
r/l
(The student had said, "My plane (/preyn/) leaves at 2:00.")
3. by pointing to wall charts posted around the classroom that signify the type of error:[4]

| -ed | | -s | | r/l | | stress | | intonation | | blending |

Obviously, the above technique can be employed only if the students understand the following rules underlying these features:
- the pronunciation of -ed and -s endings
- the difference between the articulation of /r/ and /l/
- basic word and sentence stress rules
- basic intonation patterns
- typical occasions for blending words in English

4. by having learners transcribe one portion (or all) of their recorded performance and try to locate errors *before* meeting with the teacher
5. by having learners evaluate their own recorded performance using a guide. Below are two sample guide questions to ask following a paired interview:
   a. Listen for any yes/no questions you asked. Write down two examples and describe your intonation. Was it appropriate?
   Example: Have you ever been to Disneyland?
   (rising intonation with initial rise on the first syllable of *Disneyland*)
   b. In words of more than one syllable, did you stress the proper syllable? Give five examples of such words in your talk and mark the syllable you stressed.

Peer Feedback

Having peers serve as both monitors and givers of feedback helps all students to benefit from classroom interaction, sharpen their own listening skills, and put their knowledge of pronunciation rules to immediate use. If a learner is unable to self-correct, the teacher should try to elicit the correction from a classmate. A more structured type of peer feedback can be organized in the following ways:

1. During focused exercises, learners can work in pairs or groups. For example, in a minimal-pair discrimination exercise, one person reads aloud while group members mark which member of the pair they have understood. Afterward, they compare notes.

Speaker says: Listeners mark:
1. Yellow is my favorite.   1. _____ is my favorite.
                                          a. Yellow
                                          b. Jello
2. I was joking.   2. I was _____ .
                                          a. choking
                                          b. joking

2. During presentations, role plays, and other activities, students can listen for the correctness of a particular feature—for example, the correct pronunciation of *-ed* endings in a past tense narrative.

Teacher Correction

Teachers can give feedback at any point during the lesson, either on the spot or immediately after a speech, role play, or other activity. Because students often lack a concrete way to retain and internalize the feedback and models used in class, teachers should ideally use an audio- or videocassette recorder.

In one audiotape technique, the oral dialog journal, the teacher and student communicate with each other on cassette tapes in much the same manner as they do in written dialog journals (see Kreeft-Peyton, 1987; Staton, Shuy, Peyton, & Reed, 1988). After an initial entry by the instructor, each student records a 3–5 minute response as homework. The teacher responds briefly to the content of the student entry and highlights a few selected patterns of pronunciation errors before returning the cassette to the student for another exchange. This method allows students to hear their own mistakes and review the teacher's corrections more than once before trying to correct them in their next entry.

In a similar way, if pronunciation tutoring is an option, students can record the tutoring session. Again, the recording allows the student to review what went on in the session and to listen to the models and feedback as often as desired.

Classroom Achievement Testing

Classroom tests measure the level of achievement of a student on specific, course-related measures. For this reason, the test content and format usually mirror class activities. Whereas diagnostic tests evaluate the learner's overall command of English pronunciation and are used for either placement or screening purposes, classroom tests focus on the material that has been taught and therefore indicate the student's progress within the context of a specific course and curriculum. Because diagnostic and classroom tests may be similar in design, the examples presented earlier could serve in many cases as classroom test items as well. In the items below, we have intentionally left out those formats already presented in the section on diagnostic tests. As in that earlier section, we now divide examples into those that assess perception and those that assess production.

Tests of Perception

Consonant and vowel discrimination. (Read on tape or by teacher)

1. In each line of four words, circle the word that has a different *initial* sound.
   a. George   give   gym   jelly
   b. choir   kite   car   city

2. In each line of four words, circle the word that has a different *vowel* sound.
   a. one   done   sung   gone
   b. could   fool   wool   took

For the following test formats, a basic knowledge of phonetics is necessary.[5]

3. Circle all the words that have an /iy/ sound.
   beat   fit   sleep   great
   elite   dream   bite   complete

4. Put the following words into the proper column according to their vowel sound.
   full   bull   run   look
   tool   mud   boot   should
   cut   mood   put   come

/u/	/uw/	/ə/

Pronunciation Pedagogy and Theory

5. Write the phonetic symbol for the *initial* sound you hear:
   (on tape or read by the teacher)
   a. (character)
   b. (sure)
6. Write the phonetic symbol for the *final* sound you hear:
   (on tape or read by the teacher)
   a. (rough)
   b. (lunch)
7. Write the phonetic symbol for the *vowel* sound you hear:
   (on tape or read by the teacher)
   a. (pen)
   b. (cap)
8. Write the word you hear in phonetic script:
   (on tape or read by the teacher)
   a. (knife)
   b. (threw)

Word stress. (Read on tape or by teacher)

1. Put the following words into the proper column according to their stress pattern. For each pattern one model word is provided.

   horrible   decision   beautiful
   executive   spaghetti   biography
   according   instrument   determine
   presented   communicate   usual

tálentèd	prodúctiòn	abílitỳ
horrible	spaghetti	executive

Sentence stress. (Read on tape or by teacher)

1. Mark the stressed words or syllables in the following dialog as you listen:
   Joe: Where are you going?
   Jim: To the movies. I want to see the new Woody Allen film.
   Joe: Oh, has he got another one out?
   Jim: Yeah, and I heard it's pretty good.

Intonation. (Read on tape or by teacher)

1. Mark the intonation in each two-line dialog below:
   A: How are you doing?
   B: Fine, thanks. And you?

   A: Are you ready to go?
   B: Sure. Just let me get my jacket.

Tests of Production

Classroom tests of production should focus on features that have been taught in class. The teacher can easily administer reading-aloud tests such as the one below that are designed to test the learner's command of blending and linking between words.

Read the following passage paying special attention to blending between words:

The student is doing his homework assignment. He missed school yesterday because he was sick and now he has to make it all up. The teacher helped him a little bit but now he's on his own!

Read the following passage paying special attention to the stress in the underlined words:

Bobby and Susie Smith are four-year-old twins. They are yelling and fighting. Mrs. Smith may have to separate them if their conduct doesn't improve. She won't permit them to watch TV unless they resolve their conflict. She will have to increase her control over their activities even if they protest. I suspect the children will rebel if the appropriate solution isn't found. They might not graduate from preschool!

Similar exercises can be designed to focus on such features as *-ed* and *-s* endings, other types of word stress, sentence stress, reduced speech, and intonation.

Formal Oral Proficiency Testing Instruments

We noted above that pronunciation is often not considered a "regular" part of the ESL/EFL curriculum but as an additional item to be taught when time and syllabus considerations permit. This attitude has apparently influenced the writers of commercial proficiency tests, many of which do not include an assessment of pronunciation skills in the overall test battery. However, teachers of pronunciation should be aware that a number of commercial tests *do* assess pronunciation either as a discrete entity or as one component in the students' overall oral proficiency profile. A brief overview of the most relevant tests is included in the Appendix.[6]

Conclusions

ESL/EFL teachers who address pronunciation in the classroom need more than a firm grounding in phonetics, a knowledge of updated methods and classroom activities, and familiarity with current pronunciation materials. They also need a thorough knowledge of assessment tools and strategies and the ability to apply them appropriately in placing students, analyzing their needs, designing curriculum, giving feedback, and measuring student achievement. All too often, even in programs that train teachers of ESL/EFL, assessment considerations take a back seat to issues of methods and materials. Teachers receive adequate guidance in how to teach a particular skill and what to teach but do not learn how to ascertain which items students most need to have emphasized or whether, after a given period of time, they have acquired a skill. The lack of literature in the field devoted to assessing pronunciation bears strong witness to the often uneven treatment given to it. Here we have dealt with the topic on a very practical level, delineating the various forms of assessment that are relevant to pronunciation and providing possible assessment formats.[7] We hope that others will address the theoretical issues underlying pronunciation assessment, such as reliability and validity, the interrelationship between perception and production, and the role of feedback in learner achievement, to mention but a few.

Notes

1. See Gilbert (1993, pp. vii–xi) for a pronunciation listening test.

2. Two very useful references for such minimal-pair sentences are Nilsen and Nilsen (1973) and Bowen (1975).

3. Wong (1987) provides numerous sources and ideas for eliciting spontaneous speech samples.

4. This technique is borrowed rather liberally from suggestopaedia, in which wall charts and posters are a standard part of the language classroom. The practice stems from a belief held by advocates of this method in peripheral learning—that students learn from elements present as reminders in the classroom environment. See Larsen-Freeman (1986) for more details on the use of peripheral learning.

5. Obviously, formats requiring a knowledge of phonetic symbols would be used only with students who had been taught a phonetic alphabet.

6. See Alderson, Krahnke, and Stansfield (1987) for a more complete overview of language proficiency tests.

7. See Celce-Murcia, Brinton, and Goodwin (in press) for additional guidance in this area.

References

Alderson, J. C., Krahnke, K., & Stansfield, C. W. (Eds.). (1987). *Reviews of English language proficiency tests.* Washington, DC: TESOL.

Bowen, J. D. (1975). *Patterns of English pronunciation.* Rowley, MA: Newbury House.

Celce-Murcia, M., Brinton, D., & Goodwin, J. (in press). *Teaching pronunciation: A reference for teachers of English as a second language.* New York: Cambridge University Press.

Gilbert, J. (1993). *Clear speech: Pronunciation and listening comprehension in North American English* (2nd ed.). New York: Cambridge University Press.

Kreeft-Peyton, J. (1987). *Dialog journal writing with limited English proficient students* (Educational Report 7). University of California, Los Angeles, Center for Language Education and Research.

Larsen-Freeman, D. (1986). *Techniques and principles in language teaching.* Oxford: Oxford University Press.

Nilsen, D. L. F., & Nilsen, A. P. (1973). *Pronunciation contrasts in English.* New York: Regents.

Prator, C. H., & Robinett, B. W. (1985). *Manual of American English pronunciation* (4th ed.). New York: Holt, Rinehart & Winston.

Staton, J., Shuy, R. W., Peyton, J. K., & Reed, L. (1988). *Dialogue journal communication. Classroom, linguistic, social and cognitive views.* Norwood, NJ: Ablex.

Wong, R. (1987). *Teaching pronunciation: Focus on English rhythm and intonation.* Englewood Cliffs, NJ: Prentice-Hall Regents.

Appendix

Basic English Skills Test (BEST). Measures basic functional language skills of limited-English-speaking adults. The test includes scores for fluency and pronunciation.

English Language Testing Services (ELTS) Examination. Assesses students' overall ability to meet academic language demands, including speaking. The test is communicatively oriented.

Ilyin Oral Interview. Assesses oral proficiency in English in a controlled picture sequence situation and provides diagnostic information on individual performance.

Interagency Language Roundtable (ILR) Oral Proficiency Interview. Formerly known as the Foreign Service Oral Interview, the test is designed to measure oral language scores in any language. Scores are given holistically according to the ILR proficiency scale. The test requires highly trained interviewers.

Royal Society of the Arts' Communicative Use of English as a Foreign Language (CUEFL) examination. Evaluates general oral proficiency against a scale consisting of levels described by characteristic linguistic or target performance features.

Test of Spoken English (TSE). Designed to test the oral English skills of graduate students and professionals. The test is based on verbal responses to tape-recorded and written stimuli. Although the TSE is given only at Test of English as a Foreign Language (TOEFL) testing centers, the TSE program also offers the Speaking Proficiency English Assessment Kit (SPEAK), which makes retired test forms from the TSE available for local placement purposes.

University of Cambridge First Certificate/Certificate of Proficiency in English. Designed to measure general English competence in intermediate to advanced students, especially for study and occupational purposes. The test includes an oral interview.

—adapted from Alderson, Krahnke, & Stansfield, 1987

— 2 —
Empowering Students With Predictive Skills

Wayne B. Dickerson
University of Illinois at Urbana-Champaign

Editorial Notes

Wayne Dickerson makes a strong case for the importance of empowerment as a strategic dimension of instruction in the pronunciation component of the ESL curriculum. He presents guidelines for setting goals for spelling and pronunciation empowerment, discusses in detail a variety of pronunciation rules teachers can use in developing a program, addresses the concerns of teachers in approaching this aspect of ESL instruction, and reiterates the importance of providing students with predictive skills for use both during and after formal instruction.

Dickerson takes the position that in preparing a curriculum for pronunciation instruction teachers must consider not just two, but three skills—the "three Ps." That is, in addition to training in *perception* (provided through attention to listening) and *production* (provided through attention to speaking), teachers must add *prediction* (with attention to rules for judging how to pronounce words and sentences). He argues that teaching prediction, though a novel concept in pronunciation teaching, is not at all unusual in other aspects of ESL instruction, citing grammar rules, spelling guidelines, and other generalizations, patterns, and rules of thumb given to students.

Dickerson then focuses on *vowel prediction rules*. To illustrate the operation of spelling patterns, he begins with a discussion of the familiar VC+e pattern. The spelling prediction rule here involves a generalization that attempts to help readers and speakers judge the sound of the spelled V as determined by two basic elements: (a) a neighboring letter, namely, the following single consonant letter, and (b) information about the position of the VC spelling before a word-final silent <e>. Next Dickerson explains that the centrality of word stress to vowel prediction is a fundamental fact about English that must be recognized in any approach to vowel prediction. Dickerson then moves on to generalize the spelling environment in order to capture the basic similarity of a diverse and broad-ranging set of phenomena, a crucial step. He illustrates in detail how such patterns can be generated by a few simple prediction rules that involve endings and vowel quality patterns (e.g., long, short, and reduced). Finally, he discusses accommodating polysyllabic words using the concepts of *Key* and *Left Syllables*.

Dickerson then turns to *stress prediction rules*. In the pedagogical prediction system he describes, the stress of nearly every word in English can be assigned by using one of several simple rules. He explains how each of these rules operates and gives examples.

Consonant prediction rules are then presented. Although many of the rules for predicting consonant sounds from spelling require no stress information, it is crucial in the pronunciation of some spelling patterns. Like vowel prediction rules, these rules use the Key Syllable and Left Syllable concepts.

Dickerson next summarizes the features that can transform instruction if teachers give students a systematic approach to the development of prediction skills: a new medium, a new attitude toward English spelling, a new mode of learning, new content, a new kind of correction, a new responsibility, a new resource, and a new kind of homework.

After addressing a number of key concerns of teachers, Dickerson concludes by reinforcing the point that learners can become self-instructors if trained to hone their skills in all three Ps: prediction, perception, and production.

J.M.

Empowering Students With Predictive Skills

One of the trends to sweep over ESL instruction in the past few years has been the effort to "empower" students, meaning in part to give them the resources they need to become lifelong language learners after their classes are finished. Teaching to empower students is now more common elsewhere in ESL curricula than it is in the area of pronunciation. Yet the need for students to continue improving the clarity of their oral language after course work ends is real and pressing. For this reason, empowerment should be a dimension of instruction in pronunciation as much as in any other part of an ESL program.

Empowerment: A Matter of Goals

The notion of empowerment in the context of pronunciation is best illustrated by the difference in goals seen in this familiar saying: "Give a man a fish and he will eat for a day. But teach a man to fish and he will eat for a lifetime." With a pronunciation spin on it, the saying becomes, "Teach someone the sounds of a word, and that person can say that word. But teach someone to predict those sounds, and that person can say any word." What is the goal of pronunciation instruction? Is it just to teach sounds, or also to teach students how to predict those sounds?

Those who teach pronunciation focus most of their activities on the first part of this rendition: "Teach someone the sounds of a word." Teachers spend a lot of time teaching students how to distinguish among sounds and to say them clearly in the context of the speech stream. And this time is well spent. Learners do need good listening skills; they must become accustomed to hearing real language with all its linking, trimming, and blending of sounds so that they can comprehend incoming messages. And students do need good mouth-management skills; it is essential that they know how to pronounce English sounds, stress, and melody accurately enough to meet listeners' expectations.

But what is the result of all this listening (perception) and speaking (production) work? That our students are not as empowered as they could be. Of what long-lasting value is it for learners to be able to distinguish -ē-[1] from other vowel sounds and articulate a well-formed -ē- but not know that -ē- is required in words such as *deceiving, allegiance, pleated,* and *extreme?* Something is missing if teachers stop with the goal of developing perception and production skills.

That is where the second part of the recasting comes in: "Teach someone to predict those sounds, and that person can say any word." The operative word here is *predict*. In addition to perception and production skills, students need prediction skills so they can use the sounds they know in the right places in the words they must say. Prediction skill is the ability to determine before speaking that, for instance, -ē- is the vowel sound needed in the words *deceiving, allegiance, pleated,* and *extreme* without first memorizing their pronunciations. Only a class that includes the development of prediction skills as an explicit goal can empower its students to say any word they encounter.

Of the three skills—perception, production, and prediction (the "three Ps")—the prediction skill is the most novel and the least transparent. The notion of prediction is not at all unusual in ESL instruction. Teachers give their students grammar rules, spelling guidelines, and other generalizations, patterns, and rules of thumb so they will know how to produce accurate language. What is novel is the use of the word *prediction* in connection with pronunciation.

The three following sections illustrate the meaning of prediction, using practical vowel, stress, and consonant rules that were designed for learners.[2] Students can apply these rules to standard orthography to predict the pronunciation of words they may never have seen before. The paper closes with a consideration of the impact such rules have on classroom procedures and some comments on teacher concerns (i.e., why some teachers are cautious about introducing predictive skills to their students).

Vowel Prediction Rules

Spelling Patterns

Some parts of a vowel prediction rule look familiar; other parts, not so familiar. The word *s-l-a-t-e*, for example, should be pronounced with the -ā- vowel, called *Long A*. How do readers know this? Perhaps because they have memorized the pronunciation of that spelling or because they expect the word to rhyme with others spelled that way, like *plate, hate, mate, rate,* and *fate*. Or perhaps they expect *s-l-a-t-e* to have a long vowel because it fits the familiar spelling pattern for long vowels, namely, one vowel letter (V) followed by one consonant letter (C) and a word-final silent <e>: VC+e.

A spelling pattern like VC+e is a generalization that attempts to help readers judge the sound of the spelled V—in this case, the <a>. Such a pattern consists of two basic elements: a neighboring letter, namely, the following single consonant letter, and information about the position of the <at> spelling, namely, before a word-final silent <e>.

To see how important position information is, take away the silent <e>, leaving <at> at the end of the word. This new position of <at> changes the sound of <a>, as the following examples show. A change of position that correlates with a change of sound leads to another spelling pattern: A VC at the end of a word suggests a lax vowel, in this case -a-, referred to as *Short A*. The pound sign (#) represents the end-of-word position.

VC+e:	sl*a*te	h*a*te	m*a*te	r*a*te	f*a*te
VC#:	sl*a*t	h*a*t	m*a*t	r*a*t	f*a*t

The VC+e and VC# patterns will seem familiar to most readers because they look a lot like patterns taught in grade-school phonics. But as the following discussion shows, true vowel prediction rules are light-years ahead of phonics patterns.[3] Three major factors place vowel prediction rules and phonics patterns on different planes of adequacy. First, most phonics instruction does not introduce the variable of stress; its patterns, therefore, cannot distinguish between full and reduced vowel sounds. Second, phonics does not treat anything but the simplest patterns. With a more robust concept of environment, vowel prediction rules accurately predict where phonics only hints at a sound correlation. Finally, phonics rarely goes beyond one-syllable words and therefore does not address the bulk of the English lexicon. The effect of making improvements in these three areas will become obvious in what follows.

Adding Stress Information

If the sound of <a> in *rate* is -ā- (because the word fits the VC+e pattern), then why do the last syllables of *pirate* and *considerate* not sound like *rate*? The reason is that *rate*, like all one-syllable words, has a stressed vowel, whereas the <ate> of *pirate* and *considerate* is unstressed. This means that the real reason the spelling *s-l-a-t-e is* pronounced with a long vowel is not simply that the word fits the VC+e spelling. Rather, it is because the VC+e is stressed, a basic point ignored in most phonics presentations.

The centrality of word stress to vowel prediction is a fundamental fact about English that any approach to vowel prediction must recognize.[4] Given a spelling pattern that carries a degree of stress, it is possible to make some useful symbol-sound generalizations about English. For example, a stressed VC+e predicts a long vowel; a stressed VC# predicts a short vowel; an unstressed VC+e predicts a reduced vowel.

Generalizing the Patterns

The addition of stress to a vowel spelling pattern takes a major step beyond phonics. Another step is to generalize the spelling environment to capture the basic similarity of a diverse and broad-ranging set of phenomena. An important generalization has already resulted from abstracting away from specific letters to the symbols V and C, representing any vowel letter and any consonant letter, respectively. But even more generalizations are possible.

The V́C+e pattern provides a good example. The same vowel sound that appears in *slate* is, of course, also found in *slated* and *slating*. That is, a final silent <e> is nothing special; it is one of a set of endings that signals that the preceding stressed vowel is long, as in these examples, where the vowel of <at> is long no matter which ending follows.

V́C+e	slate	hate	mate	rate	grate	V́C+W
V́C+ed	slated	hated	mated	rated	grated	V́C+W
V́C+ing	slating	hating	mating	rating	grating	V́C+W

I call this set of endings—*-e*, *-ed*, and *-ing*—*Weak Endings*. To capture in the pattern the similar behavior of all these endings, the specific position markers, +e, +ed, and +ing, can be replaced with the general +W, which means a position before a Weak Ending. V́C+W, given above on the right of each line, characterizes all these words.

Generalizing the application of +W moves even further away from phonics. In fact, *-e*, *-ed*, and *-ing* are not that special, either; English has quite a few Weak Endings, about 40 in all. In the examples given below a subscript wedge (ᴀ) separates the ending from the rest of the word. The familiar <at> is in the items in the first row and before other Weak Endings, like *-al*, *-er*, *-able*, and so on. If these are Weak Endings, too, then the <at> in these words should fit the V́C+W pattern for long vowels, as indeed it does. Below the <at> set are even more words with Weak Endings, namely, *-er*, *-ar*, *-en*, *-ary*, *-est*, *-ive*, and so on. In these examples, the VC has not been restricted to <at>. Nevertheless, the V in the V́C+W pattern is long:

fátᴀal	crátᴀer	státᴀable	látᴀest	nátᴀure	látᴀent
A	E	I	O		U
rácᴀer	cédᴀar	rípᴀen	rótᴀary		cútᴀest
nátᴀive	évᴀen	sízᴀable	mótᴀor		fútᴀure
látᴀency	légᴀal	vírᴀus	pótᴀent		cúbᴀoid
blátᴀant	vénᴀous	írᴀis	óvᴀum		brútᴀal

Summarizing the main points so far: Vowel letters have no sounds unless they are embedded in a spelling environment and are accompanied by stress information.[5] Any particular instance of this fact, such as "a vowel letter in a stressed vowel-consonant string before a Weak Ending represents a long vowel," can be reduced to its essence, as noted in the first formula below. A spelling-stress combination is written to the left of the equals (=) sign, and a vowel quality is written to the right. The equals sign is read as *predicts*: "A stressed VC+W predicts long." If that same spelling is unstressed, the pattern predicts a reduced vowel—the quick, quiet vowel heard in the last syllable of *pirate* and *considerate*. That is the second formula. A stressed VC at the end of a word predicts a short vowel, as captured in the third formula. These formulas are *vowel quality patterns*. They are prediction rules; they are empowerment rules.

V́C+W = long   V̌C+W = reduced   V́C# = short

To use such patterns to predict specific long, short, and reduced vowel sounds, a student must examine a word to determine which of the already-memorized vowel quality patterns matches the environment of the vowel letter in question. Having found a match, the student then uses the Symbol Generating Mechanism to mechanically generate a specific vowel symbol for the target vowel. For example, if the word is *flake*, the learner would note that the pattern, V́C+W = long, matches the environment of the target vowel in this word, because all single-syllable words carry stress. This match is noted below as arrow 1. The correlation between V́C+W and a vowel quality prediction (represented by arrow 2) is the vowel quality pattern a student memorizes beforehand. At this point the learner generates a specific vowel symbol by taking the shape of the symbol from the spelling (arrow 3) and adding to the symbol a long mark (macron) because the vowel quality pattern predicts "long" (arrow 4).[6]

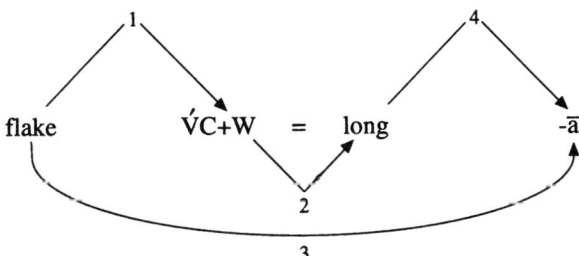

Students learn these vowel quality patterns and learn them well, even beginners. Intermediate and advanced students practice the patterns with word sets and exercises that are different from those that beginners use. Even so, according to their needs students at all levels can profit from prediction patterns.

Although students use such patterns mainly as a resource for their own self-correction during their periods of private language practice, rules occasionally surface in interaction. One of my students reported an encounter at a grocery store where he asked a stock boy for -kon flaks-. After repeated, unsuccessful attempts to get the stock boy to understand, my student reported pausing, thinking about his words, noticing that one of his words fit the stressed VC+W pattern, and changing his speech to match his prediction: -kon flāks-, whereupon he was directed to the aisle for cereals.[7]

Accommodating Polysyllabic Words

When written with the appropriate environment, vowel quality patterns empower students to predict the sound of any vowel in any word, regardless of its length. This is another feature that puts vowel quality patterns a great distance ahead of phonics patterns with respect to their predictive capabilities. An example follows.

The V́C+W pattern works with all the words in the last section because the stress is on the VC syllable just to the left of the Weak Ending; the pattern maps directly and unambiguously onto such words. But what if the stress is not on the syllable just to the left of the Weak Ending? What about a word like *sabbátical*, in which the stress is not next to the -*al* Weak Ending? Will vowel quality patterns still work? The answer is yes. All that is required is to choose the right pattern, that is, the pattern with the environment that matches that of the target vowel. If the target vowel is in the unstressed *ic* left of -*al* (marked with a single underline below), then V̆C+W = reduced fits the vowel and accurately predicts the sound as schwa: -səbatəkəl-. As for the stressed vowel in the syllable left of the *ic* (marked with a double underline), its pattern will become clear when some of the syllables in the word are labeled.

sabbátic▴al

In words with Weak Endings of the sort illustrated above and below, the syllable immediately to the left of the ending is called the *Key Syllable*; it always begins with a vowel letter, as underlined with a single stroke in the word above and in those that follow. The syllable just to the left of the Key Syllable is called the *Left Syllable* (marked with a double underline). The process of finding the Key and Left Syllables is mechanical. With practice, students become very adept at identifying these spelled syllables in all kinds of words.

Vátic▴an	plátin▴um	fanátic▴al	láter▴al
A	E	I	O
grádu▴al	strénu▴ous	contínu▴um	innócu▴ous
calámit▴ous	médic▴al	clínic▴al	hippopótam▴us
análys▴is	skélet▴on	mílit▴ant	hómic▴ide
plánet▴oid	régim▴en	mínim▴um	abdómin▴al

The Left Syllable <at> in *Vatican, platinum, fanatical,* and *lateral* is pronounced as Short A, as are all the Left Syllable vowels in the words listed under A, E, I, and O. This is because they exemplify a pattern that predominates in the English language: Stressed VCs in Left Syllables have short vowels—except when the vowel is spelled <u>, as in *númerous, alúminum, cúmulus,* and *fúneral,* in which the Left Syllable vowel is long.

Stating these powerful generalizations requires indicating the new position of the VC, namely, in the Left Syllable (a left-pointing arrow is the position marker). Thus, a V́C← predicts short whereas úC← predicts long, as the vowel quality patterns below advertise.[8] The úC← pattern is a *specific* vowel quality pattern because it is written with a specific vowel letter. It contrasts with *general* vowel quality patterns, like V́C←, which are written with the general V. As an important matter of convention, specific patterns apply before general patterns; this allows úC← to filter out the <u> spellings before V́C← applies. When a Left Syllable pattern is found to apply, whether long or short, the Symbol Generating Mechanism works in the way described above to generate a symbol for the sound predicted.

úC← = long   V́C← = short

The sampling of vowel prediction rules in this section has illustrated the important differences between phonics patterns and vowel quality patterns. Vowel quality patterns consist of a spelling pattern and a degree of stress on the left and a vowel prediction on the right. A close look at a spelling pattern reveals that it has three elements: the vowel letter or letters of the target sound, relevant consonant letters in the environment, and relevant position markers. The left side of the pattern, then, shows what is distinctive about vowel quality patterns in general: (a) Stress is an integral part of the rule; (b) robust environmental information is incorporated into the rule to make it as exact and yet as generally applicable as possible; and (c) position information allows learners to predict vowel sounds anywhere in a word— in Key Syllables, Left Syllables, and elsewhere—regardless of word length.

Stress Prediction Rules

The success of vowel quality patterns rests in large measure on a student's ability to judge the location of word stress. A student knows whether a word is stressed on the Left Syllable or on the Key Syllable by learning orthography-based stress rules.

In the pedagogical prediction system described here, the stress of nearly every word in English can be assigned by using one of four simple rules. To illustrate what a stress rule looks like and how it works, the following discussion will focus on only one of the four, the V/VC Weak Stress Rule.

Each stress rule applies to its own domain—its own sets of words. The V/VC Weak Stress Rule applies to words that have the following endings, called V/VC Weak Endings: *-al, -an, -ant, -ance, -ancy, -en$_N$, -ent, -ence, -ency, -ide, -is, -ite, -oid, -on, -ous, -um, -us*. The subscript N following *-en* means that only the *-en* of nouns is a V/VC Weak Ending.[9]

The V/VC Weak Stress Rule, like the other three rules, begins at the Key Syllable and asks the user to evaluate it. In fact, one of the meanings of the label *Weak* is that evaluation is required: whether or not the Key is spelled with a V (a single vowel letter with no following consonant letter) or with a VC. In the word list in the last section, examples of V Keys are underlined with a single stroke in the first row under A, E, I, and O (*gradual, strenuous*, etc.), and examples of VC Keys fill the following rows (*calamitous, medical*, etc.) and the <at> set across the top (*Vatican, platinum*, etc.). If either of these spellings appears in the Key, then the word stress will be on the Left Syllable, as in all these examples. If, however, the Key is spelled in any other way, stress must remain on the Key. In the following words, the VV and VCC Keys retain the stress.[10]

flambóy▲ant	cubóid▲al	amóeb▲oid	abýsm▲al
momént▲um	treménd▲ous	patérn▲al	tobógg▲an
prospéct▲us	persímm▲on	synóps▲is	reminísc▲ent

The V/VC Weak Stress Rule, then, requires the user to evaluate the Key Syllable to determine whether or not it is spelled with a single V or a VC. Stress placement proceeds on the basis of the evaluation. The rule is given below in its formal form (Dickerson, 1989, unit 3, pp. 24ff). "If you cannot Stress Left" refers to two situations: either there is no Left Syllable or there is no V or VC in the Key. Both situations are illustrated in the list above.

V/VC Weak Stress Rule
From a V or VC Key, Stress Left.
If you cannot Stress Left, Stress Key.

Students using the textbook by Dickerson (1989a) encounter the V/VC Weak Stress Rule only after they have learned to identify Key and Left Syllables and to use vowel quality patterns. By the time they learn this rule, they can focus exclusively on making word-stress predictions and on using those predictions as the basis for their well-rehearsed vowel quality patterns.

Consonant Prediction Rules

Most rules to predict consonant sounds from spelling require no information on stress. But in words like the following, the pronunciation of the consonant just before the Key (underlined) depends directly on word stress. Here the V/VC Weak Stress Rule applies, placing stress on the Left Syllable because of a V or VC Key. This leaves the Key Syllable unstressed, which figures importantly in the prediction.

t	d	Cs	Vs	x
impétu͜ous	assídu͜ous	íssu͜ance	cásu͜al	séxu͜al
constítu͜ent	procédur͜al	sénsu͜ous	vísu͜al	fléxur͜al

Depending on their region, English speakers pronounce the target <t> in the first column as -ty- or -ch-, the <d> in the second column as -dy- or -j-, the <s> after a consonant letter in the third column as -sy- or -sh-, the <s> after a vowel letter in the fourth column as -zy- or -zh-, and the <x> in the last column as -ksy- or -ksh-. Both pronunciations in each case are educated English.

The kind of variation seen in the pronunciation of <t, d, s> and <x> in these words occurs everywhere in English before the letter <u> when it represents an unstressed vowel. Hence the importance of stress. To identify the <u> more precisely, note that it can occur anywhere except in a VC# or a VCC spelling pattern, as in *consul* or *August*. This <u> is what we call a *y-ful spelling* because it invites a -y- consonant to precede it, as in the first variant of each pair of pronunciations above. In some regions, the /y/ is preserved (e.g., -tisyū- for *tissue*), whereas in others, it disappears in the palatal assimilation of the alveolar consonants represented by <t, d, s> and <x> (e.g., -tishū- for *tissue*).

Prediction patterns for consonants are called *consonant-correspondence* (or *con-cor*) *patterns*. To state the con-cor patterns for <t, d, s> and <x>, the y-ful spelling is abbreviated to YS and a breve indicates that this vowel spelling is unstressed.[11] Again, the left side of the pattern represents spelling information, and the right side represents the sound prediction, just as in a vowel quality pattern. A slash (/) separates the two educated variants and means *or*.

t + Y̆S = -ty/ch-   d + Y̆S = -dy/j -
Cs + Y̆S = -sy/sh-   Vs + Y̆S = -zy/zh-
x + Y̆S = -ksy/ksh-

Y-ful spellings participate in other con-cor patterns, too, such as those that account for the optional presence of -y- in words like *tune, duty,* and *nude,* for the obligatory absence of -y- in words like *rude, June,* and *clue,* and for the obligatory presence of -y- before all other y-ful spellings, as in *mule, cute,* and *fume*. The complete system of YS con-cor patterns can be found in Dickerson (1985); the pedagogical presentation of these rules is given in Dickerson (1989a, unit 3, pp. 33–42).

Instructional Consequences of Teaching for Empowerment

Students who are empowered in pronunciation are capable of continuing to improve the accuracy, clarity, and intelligibility of their oral English after formal instruction ends. To equip students with this capability means adding prediction activities to standard production and perception activities. If done systematically so that prediction skills develop in all areas of the sound system, adding these activities radically transforms instruction.

1. By adding orthography-based prediction to pronunciation work, teachers add *a new medium* to classroom instruction. Students receive visual-graphic stimuli rather than only oral-aural, as written words become a new and valuable source of information about the sound system.

2. A systematic and broad-ranging presentation of symbol-sound patterns engenders *a new attitude toward English spelling*. Instead of siding with critics who deride English spelling as irrational and hopelessly inadequate, students learn firsthand that the spelling system is overwhelmingly regular. If it were not so, prediction rules of the kind illustrated above either would not be possible or would not be so useful. Acknowledging the exceptions, learners focus on the value to be found in the pervasive regularity that exists. In effect, they take the same healthy point of view as those who do not stop learning the past tense just because the simple past of *to be* is *was*, the past of *to go* is *went*, and the past of many common verbs is a strong form. They simply memorize the few highly visible lapses, treating them as incidental, and move on to the predominant patterns that characterize the bulk of the system.[12]

3. By empowering students in pronunciation, teachers naturally engage their students in *a new mode of learning*, emphasizing cognitive activities in addition to behavioral activities. Learners are challenged to understand how orthography and the sound system work and to use that information to inform their speech. Teachers thereby challenge those who learn best through analysis without diminishing opportunities for those who learn best through active involvement in speaking.

4. *New content* also surfaces. Teachers are serious about using rules to predict word stress, vowels, consonants, and so on. Although novel to most students, rules as subject matter complement the articulatory subject matter. Furthermore, students welcome this new content. Every new lesson offers a surprise and a revelation about the patterning of orthography, and every new lesson increases the students' personal control over the sound system.

5. In class, prediction also places a priority on *a new kind of correction*—self-correction. For example, when a student says *abdominal* with a Long O, teachers do not say, "That's not quite it. It's *abdominal* [using a Short O]. Repeat after me." Rather, they elicit self-correction: "Let's look at that again. Your stress is right, but which vowel quality pattern applies to a stressed Left Syllable? That's right, it's V́C← = short. So which short vowel is required? Now, say the word again." Teachers guide students to use this kind of self-inspection and self-correction, and students guide each other in the same way. When asked to do so, they take the role of the instructor to help their peers to self-discovery. This is an effective way to get students to learn the set of queries (self-inspection questions) that can lead to self-correction (Morley, 1991, p. 503).

6. A focus on prediction also adds *a new responsibility*. Learners no longer have to wait for the teacher to teach them, nor do they have to confine their learning to the classroom, because prediction skills empower learners to teach themselves at any time in any location. They have the tools with which to become self-instructors. The teacher's task is to encourage them to recognize and take on that responsibility (Morley, 1991, pp. 494, 503).

7. Prediction from orthography contributes *a new resource* to students for self-correction. When they monitor their speech during private covert rehearsal, they have both a memory of how a sound is formed and a rule-based guidance system to figure out for themselves what a sound should be. After attempting a new pronunciation, students can verify their stress, vowel, or consonant choice by reflecting on the pattern that governs the stress, vowel, or consonant in question.

8. Finally, an emphasis on prediction creates *a new kind of homework* for those working on their pronunciation. Beyond language lab assignments, which are important for concentrated work on targets that have been presented but not yet internalized, pencil-and-paper exercises give students practice using rules to make predictions. Then, by producing their own tape recordings, they demonstrate that they can indeed guide and shape their production by the predictions they make.

Concerns of Teachers

For all the exciting possibilities noted above, teaching for empowerment can wrench a classroom out of its comfortable mold. Are teachers ready? What are their concerns?

The best teaching is teaching that meets needs. Teaching to empower students in pronunciation is not only a reasonable aim of instruction, but, because it meets students' needs, it should also be an obligatory aim. More than a decade of teaching and research has shown that such an aim is clearly achievable. Yet over the years ESL teachers have voiced a variety of misgivings about the feasibility and even the wisdom of incorporating prediction work into their curricula. I address some of these apprehensions here.

One concern is well founded: Materials are not yet available for all levels of students. Although more materials are coming, teachers interested in developing prediction components for lessons directed to low- and low-intermediate-level students may have to adapt the content of more advanced texts, such as Dickerson (1989a), which are written for upper-intermediate and advanced students. The generalizations are applicable to all levels, but the exercise materials must be adjusted to suit the competence of lower-level students.[13]

Other concerns are not so well founded. For instance, some teachers feel that the prediction goal, if adopted at all, should be reserved for more advanced students; lower-level students should focus on production and perception. Experience indicates otherwise; prediction is appropriate for adult students at all levels of competence. In fact, prediction and production skills grow best when they grow together from the start because they are interdependent. To be able to articulate a sound but not to know that it is required in a particular word is only half a victory, as is being able to predict that a sound is required in a word but unable to articulate the predicted sound.

Some teachers may be apprehensive if prediction information looks complicated; they may feel it will be very difficult to learn. Prediction patterns will look strange to teachers and students alike, yet the rules were designed for linguistically unsophisticated learners; their form belies their simplicity. Because students master the rules quickly given adequate practice, their teachers can be assured they can do the same. At the beginning, all teachers need to do is stay 1 class hour ahead of their students (Dickerson, 1984).

Another criticism is that learning rules is too much like linguistics, in which the focus is on learning about the language, not learning the language itself. Yet knowledge and skill are inseparable in language. In every speaker, language competence and language performance go hand in hand; speakers are able to speak because their tacit sense of how the system works guides their use of language. In most cases, the intuitions of learners about the L2 are lacking or wrong. Formal rules of pronunciation, like formal rules of grammatical structure, are surrogates for those intuitions and help them develop so that the L2 user can make good judgments when using the new language (Dickerson, 1987b). Prediction rules do indeed contain information about the language. But their reason for being is to guide language learning, not to instruct students in the esoterica of linguistics. Without such rules, learners are seriously handicapped.

Still other critics say that too little time is available for pronunciation work to launch into a system of rules that could never be completely taught. Granted, the prediction system with its various patterns may look imposing. The fact remains, however, that the system is not a house of cards; rules can be extracted from the whole. Vowel, consonant, and stress rules apply to their own narrowly defined domains and, as such, can be introduced in any one of those domains alone. For example, although the V/VC Weak Stress rule governs the stress of about 20 word sets, attention to just one set, such as -*ous*, is an opportunity to teach the stress rule. Similarly, when working on the articulation of the voiced and voiceless tip-dental fricatives, -TH- and -th-, it is appropriate to present the con-cor patterns that show students how to tell whether <th> is voiced or voiceless, even if no other con-cor patterns are discussed (Dickerson, 1987b). The value of the rule system is not diminished by presenting only a few rules as time permits. The gain is that students learn a powerful self-help tool each time they encounter a rule, regardless of the number of such rules that can be covered.

Finally, in an era of communicative language teaching with its concern for appropriate input, some teachers feel that rule work is a distraction from what is really more important, namely, using language in interaction. Although this emphasis is a healthy antidote to communicatively meaningless language activities, the emphasis recognizes only the public (interactive) side of language learning and ignores the important private (introspective) side, where language skills are developed (Avery & Ehrlich, 1992, pp. 215–219; Stevick, 1980, p. 279). Formal rules do not belong to the public side; they have no place in communicative encounters in which the message itself, more than the form of the message, dominates. Instead, rules are for use in private when learners, off by themselves, go over L2 speech in their heads, think about the structure of their utterances, evaluate the accuracy of their articulations, and rehearse their improved renditions, anticipating their use in public. Rule work, then, is not a distraction from more important matters but one of the principal ways learners build up their repertoire of tools to use to shape their private speech so that their public speech will be more intelligible (Dickerson, 1987b).

Conclusion

Teaching pronunciation for empowerment means teaching learners how to teach themselves during periods of covert rehearsal (Dickerson, 1987a). To create such self-instructors involves honing learners' skills in the three Ps—prediction, perception, and production. I have attempted to show what some pronunciation rules look like, have identified the impact on instruction that teachers can expect if they decide to use prediction rules in class, and have tried to allay their concerns if they are uncertain about doing so.

Although I have focused on orthography-based rules, I do not mean to imply that pedagogical rules are only of this kind. Indeed, if they were, the system would be limited to word-level phonology (consonants, vowels, and word stress). Phrase-level rules for good rhythm, correct sentence and construction stress, and meaningful intonation are also part of a thorough prediction-oriented syllabus (Dickerson, 1989a). Rather, my intent in concentrating on orthography-based rules has been twofold: first, to draw a clear distinction between phonics rules as seen in ESL materials and versatile prediction rules (a wide gap in adequacy separates the two) and, second, to emphasize again that the English spelling system, for all its highly visible anomalies, nevertheless paints a quite faithful picture of English (word-level) phonology.[14] But whether they look at word-level or phrase-level rules, the message to teachers is the same: Their task should be to equip students with those liberating skills that enable them to evaluate and modify their own pronunciations for the rest of their English-speaking careers. That is teaching for empowerment.

Notes

1. To facilitate the prediction of sounds from spelling, pronunciation classes at the University of Illinois at Urbana-Champaign use a transcription system in which the symbols look much like standard letters of the alphabet and have familiar values. To avoid confusion between these "pedagogical" symbols and others used to represent vowel and consonant phonemes, we place our symbols between dashes, e.g., -ē-. The following pedagogical symbols appear in this paper and correspond to symbols that students and teachers may be more familiar with: -ē- (/iː, iy/), -i- (/ɪ, i/), -ā- (/eɪ, ey/), -a- (/æ/), -ō- (/əʊ, ow/), -o- (/ɒ, ɑː, ɑ/), -ə- (/ə/ unstressed only), -ū- (/uː, uw/), -th- (/θ/), -TH- (/ð/), -sh- (/ʃ, š/), -zh- (/ʒ, ž/), -ch- (/tʃ, tš, č/), -j- (/dʒ, dž, ǰ/), -y- (/j, y/). Other pedagogical symbols used here are not ambiguous: -t, d, k, f, v, s, z, n, m, l, r-. For a discussion of the rationale and structure of the pedagogical vowel and consonant charts used in our work, see Dickerson (1992; 1989b, unit 1, pp. 6–9). See also Wang (1991) for a non-Western view on orthography-based symbols.

2. All the rules discussed in this paper have been used since the 1980s to teach English pronunciation at the University of Illinois at Urbana-Champaign. They are presented in pedagogical form, with oral and written exercises, in Dickerson (1989a). The teacher's manual that accompanies the student text (Dickerson, 1989b) contains lesson-planning suggestions, oral and written tests, section reviews, answers to all exercises and quizzes, and an abundance of practical suggestions as well as less widely available background information. A set of cassette tape recordings with 52 10-minute segments, covering all the lessons in the text, is also available from the publisher.

3. The reason for raising this contrast is that numerous ESL texts purport to help learners use English spelling as a guide to pronunciation by taking the phonics

approach (e.g., Kirn, 1991; McClelland, Hale, & Beaudikofer, 1979; Sevastopoulos, 1981). These texts promise more than they can deliver because of the inherent limitations of phonics as described here. Unfortunately, many ESL pronunciation texts also take a phonics approach to the symbol-sound information they provide the learner.

4. Phonics attempts to avoid the problem of word stress by restricting vocabulary to mainly monosyllabic items. Because monosyllabic words carry major stress, phonics patterns are exclusively for full vowels in the final (and only) syllable. There are no patterns for reduced vowels—the bulk of vowel sounds in running text—nor for most vowel sounds in nonfinal position.

5. This is why the spelling hints offered in so many ESL pronunciation texts are next to worthless, whether they are the two stressless patterns for "long" and "short" vowels or more often the stressless and environmentless list of spellings that happen to be pronounced somewhere in English with a particular vowel sound, for example, <a, ai, ay, ea, ei, ey> as spellings for the -ā-vowel.

6. In the case of a short vowel quality pattern, no macron is added to the symbol shape taken from the spelling. If the prediction is "reduced," the Symbol Generating Mechanism simply converts "reduced" to schwa, -ə-. Other refinements are summarized in Dickerson (1989a, unit 1, p. 159).

7. Besides Weak Endings, students also watch for Neutral Endings, such as the final -s in *flakes*. Neutral Endings are ignored for vowel quality purposes. That is, the word *flakes* is treated as if it were *flake*.

8. The technical origins of this pair of patterns and their pedagogical application are discussed in Dickerson (1980), and an ESL introduction to the patterns is presented in Dickerson (1989a, unit 2, pp. 119–128).

9. Other Weak Endings introduced earlier, such as *-able, -ar, -ary, -e, -ed, -en, -er, -est, -ing, -ive, -or,* and *-ure,* are examples of Prefix Weak Endings and are signals to use the Prefix Weak Stress Rule. See Dickerson (1989b, unit 2, pp. 97–106) for a pedagogical introduction to this rule. All Prefix Weak and V/VC Weak Endings are introduced to students gradually—usually only two or three per lesson.

10. The <y> in the word *flamboyant* is a vowel letter, as are all instances of <y> immediately after a vowel letter.

11. YS also stands for other y-ful spellings, namely, <eu> and <ew>, which behave exactly as <u> spellings do. The <u> of <au> and <ou>, however, is not considered a YS.

12. Particularly for Chinese students, the sound-prediction system introduced here constitutes a revelation that regularity of any kind exists in English orthography. They learned to spell English words by memorizing English spellings; they read English by recognizing memorized word shapes, just as they do with their own Chinese characters. Assuming no symbol-sound relationships, they found none and proceeded as if the letters of the Roman alphabet were as arbitrarily related to sounds as their Chinese characters are (Wang, 1991).

13. Often the most difficult part of adapting a higher-level lesson to lower-level students is finding appropriate vocabulary with which to build the lesson. One source of words ready at hand is the electronic dictionary associated with word processors.

In many such dictionaries, the *find* or *look up* function allows a user to search for all words of a particular kind, such as all words that end in *-ous*. Most also allow the user to print out the word lists generated in this way.

14. The importance of continuing to claim that English orthography is superbly well-formed cannot be underestimated. Ignorance of how the English spelling system works is epidemic even among those who should know. Citing only one example from dozens, I quote from one of the newest teacher-preparation texts on the market, in which misinformation is passed on to a new generation of teachers (Avery & Ehrlich, 1992):

> The English spelling system often fails to represent the sounds of English in a straightforward manner. In other words, there is often no one-to-one correspondence between the sounds that we hear and the letters we see on a page. An examination of the English spelling system reveals many examples of this discrepancy between spelling and sound. (p. 3)

Assuming that English spelling is based on the principle of one-to-one symbol-sound correspondences, the authors note its "failing" to live up to this ideal because of many "discrepancies." The problem with this quotation is that the assumption is wrong; English spelling is not based on the one-to-one principle and should not be faulted for not living up to its standards. English orthography is a morphophonemic system in which letters relate to sounds (phonemes) in the context of words (morphemes). That is precisely the principle that vowel quality patterns and con-cor patterns claim for English orthography. See "How English Orthography Works, An Essay" (Dickerson, 1989a, unit 3, pp. 141–146), for a discussion of this point.

References

Avery, P., & Ehrlich, S. (1992). *Teaching American English pronunciation.* New York: Oxford University Press.

Dickerson, W. B. (1980). Bisyllabic laxing rule: Vowel prediction in linguistics and language learning. *Language Learning, 30,* 317–329. (Erratum, 1981, *Language Learning, 31,* 283.)

Dickerson, W. B. (1984). The role of formal rules in pronunciation instruction. In J. Handscombe, R. Orem, & B. Taylor (Eds.), *On TESOL '83* (pp. 135–148). Washington, DC: TESOL.

Dickerson, W. B. (1985). The invisible Y: A case for spelling in pronunciation learning. *TESOL Quarterly, 19,* 303–316.

Dickerson, W. B. (1987a). Explicit rules and the developing interlanguage phonology. In A. James & J. Leather (Eds.), *Sound patterns in second language acquisition* (pp. 121–140). Amsterdam: Foris.

Dickerson, W. B. (1987b). Orthography as a pronunciation resource. *World Englishes, 6,* 11–20. (Reprinted in A. Brown [Ed.]., 1991, *Teaching English pronunciation: A book of readings* [pp. 159–172]. London: Routledge.)

Dickerson, W. B. (1989a). *Stress in the speech stream: The rhythm of spoken English student text.* Urbana: University of Illinois Press.

Dickerson, W. B. (1989b). *Stress in the speech stream: The rhythm of spoken English teacher's manual.* Urbana: University of Illinois Press.

Dickerson, W. B. (1992). Orthography: A window on the world of sound. In A. Brown (Ed.), *Approaches to pronunciation teaching* (pp. 103–117). New York: Macmillan.

Kirn, H. E. (1991). *Practical everyday spelling workbook: Patterns and principles of English spelling.* Lincolnwood, IL: National Textbook.

McClelland, L., Hale, P. A., & Beaudikofer, D. (1979). *English sounds and spelling.* Englewood Cliffs, NJ: Prentice-Hall.

Morley, J. (1991). The pronunciation component in teaching English to speakers of other languages. *TESOL Quarterly, 25,* 481–520.

Sevastopoulos, J. (1981). *Keys to spelling, sounds and syllables.* Silver Spring, MD: Institute of Modern Languages.

Stevick, E. (1980). *A way and ways.* Rowley, MA: Newbury House.

Wang, H. S. (1991). An orthography-based symbolic system for TESL. *English Teaching Forum, 29,* 16–21.

— 3 —
Intonation: A Navigation Guide for the Listener (and gadgets to help teach it)

Judy B. Gilbert
University of California, Berkeley Extension

Editorial Notes

Judy Gilbert suggests three changes in pronunciation teaching that would make it more effective:

1. using methods other than mechanical drill or memorized rules to make students aware of concepts
2. emphasizing the "musical" aspects of pronunciation more than individual sounds
3. contextualizing the teaching point within real speech and providing practice in efficient guessing about the implications of discourse signals.

In the balance of the paper, Gilbert presents some practical suggestions for teachers on topics to teach and ways to teach them.

Gilbert discusses four building blocks of intonation and outlines a minilesson for each. In the section on *linking* she reminds teachers that, unlike printed English, spoken English often contains no white space to indicate the separation of words. That is, words run together in sequences of sounds, with little or no perceptible pausing until the end of the phrase or short utterance. This phenomenon, she notes, is an especially important feature of spoken English that needs special attention in the pronunciation curriculum. Next she presents some salient features of *word rhythm* and some exercise prototypes. Sections on *sentence rhythm* and *melody* follow.

Gilbert draws attention to important aspects of the main purpose of intonation: *helping the listener to follow.* In discussing English emphasis she observes that discourse signals keep the conversation on track; that is, the emphases and pauses in the discourse serve as directional guides that help the listener follow the conversation. She discusses the function of sentence emphasis in terms of old information and new information and notes that in English intonation is the primary means by which speakers give special importance to particular words; this is done via a system that works by contrast—emphasis and deemphasis. Next she emphasizes the importance of *the learner's own words* and advocates shifting students from a practice format that involves repetition to one that provides students with opportunities to use intonation interactively. Her examples of contextualized practices involve students in making predictions and require students to attend to the orientation of the conversation by utilizing previously given information.

Gilbert notes that English speakers help their listeners to follow the conversation not only by contrastive emphasis, but by grouping words into *thought groups* so that they can be processed more easily. She points out the importance of the prominent word, or *focus word*, in each thought group as well as falling pitches and pauses as markers for the end of a thought group.

In concluding, Gilbert claims that by teaching linking, rhythm, stress, and intonation, teachers place pronunciation teaching in a more communicative setting. She urges the use of a variety of modalities in instruction—kinesthetic, visual, aural—that will enable students to sharpen their ability to attend to key features of pronunciation.

J.M.

Intonation: A Navigation Guide for the Listener[1]
(and gadgets to help teach it)

Pronunciation has been something of an orphan in English programs around the world. Yet thoughtful teachers have been well aware that this neglect has been unwise: "We have probably all met foreign speakers of English who sounded very fluent and may have been perfectly grammatical, with appropriate vocabulary, but who were unintelligible owing to poor pronunciation" (Brown, 1991, p. 1); "A pause in the wrong place, an intonation misunderstood, and a whole conversation went awry" (Forster, 1924/1951, p. 274).

Why has pronunciation been a poor relation? I think it is because the subject has been drilled to death, with too few results from too much effort. Both teachers and students generally assume that pronunciation can improve only through the disciplined practice of individual sounds. That is why it seemed reasonable that Eliza Doolittle would achieve perfection by submitting to lengthy bullying, "practice makes perfect" being the guiding principle. The trouble with this picture is that it does not seem to work very well.

I suggest three kinds of change:

1. more concern for ways to arouse alert attention to a concept to be understood, as opposed to mechanical drill or a rule to be memorized

2. more attention to the "musical" aspects of pronunciation (rhythm and intonation) and less to individual sounds

3. more time spent fitting the teaching point into real speech, especially including practice in efficient guessing about the implications of discourse signals.

As Brazil, Coulthard, and Johns (1980) have noted, "At a time when communicative competence has emerged as a goal for the language learner, it would seem that the time is ripe for considering ways of integrating the teaching of intonation . . . into the language syllabus" (p. 117).

Building Blocks of Intonation

Following are some suggestions for topics to teach and methods for teaching them.

Linking

Beginning students of French are always taught about *liaison*, the way words run together. This concept is considered essential both for the production of understandable French and for listening comprehension. Oddly enough, students of ESL are not usually taught about liaison, but in fact English also runs words together, that is, links them in certain ways. Ignorance of linking badly affects both speech clarity and listening comprehension. Unlike printed English, spoken English contains no white space separating words. Nonnative listeners, expecting this separation, will have difficulty recognizing separate words, so that they might interpret *all of* as *a love* or reach some equally confusing conclusion. In reality only novice ESL teachers, eager to be helpful, speak with white spaces between words.

Gadget: Magnets. One way to introduce linking vividly is with magnets. The pull of the magnet is a physical metaphor to wake up the class and fix a memory of the point being taught. Unlike other gadgets discussed here, this one requires some preparation time. The metaphor is the irresistible attraction between succeeding words, especially if the following word begins with a vowel. A strong magnet and a piece of iron are needed to produce this effect. The teacher paints or presses vinyl letters onto a block of wood for the first word (e.g., *AT*) and glues the magnet onto the end of the block. A styrene-based adhesive works best for gluing metal to wood. Then a piece of flat iron is glued onto the facing end of the second word (e.g., *ALL*).

When presented with this peculiar word, *ATALL* (or *GOOUT*), the students will be puzzled. If the teacher pulls the blocks apart, the words are easy to read: *AT ALL* and *GO OUT*. When the two words get close enough for the attraction to occur, they snap together with a bang that resonates with the meaning of the lesson. The difficulty of *reading* run-together words mimics the difficulty of *hearing* run-together words. Students are apt to remember this physical image.

A simpler way to call attention to linking is with a pencil: The teacher draws a curved line (like the bottom of a link) between the last and first letters.

Minilesson. Draw a linking mark to connect these words.

Examples:

(Continuant to vowel)
wi th‿all / thi s‿ice / pro ve‿it

(Stop to vowel)
can' t‿always / ro b‿us / than k‿you (thank Q)

(Continuant to continuant)
bu s‿system / tea m‿members / ha ve‿made

Word Rhythm

Why is it valuable to teach rhythm? Abberton, Parker, and Fourcin (1978), working with speech improvement for deaf adults, reported one especially salient feature: They are more likely to form individual sounds clearly if the sounds are said in the correct rhythmic patterns of the new language. Wong (1987) identified a number of critical features of rhythm that are important in ESL instruction:

> With young children, music, rhymes, and storytelling can be exploited for their wealth of rhythmic examples without resorting to explicit treatments of the phenomenon. Adult learners, however, will benefit from conscious attention to the features of rhythm: syllable length, stressed syllables, full and reduced vowels, pauses, linking and blending sounds between words, and how words are made prominent by accenting syllables and simultaneously lengthening syllables. (p. 24)

People learn the rhythm of language in infancy and thereafter apply it unconsciously to their own language or any other they are learning. Many languages have rhythm patterns based on the roughly equal length of syllables (e.g., Japanese and Spanish). English, however, has a rhythm based on variation in syllable length. One of the most significant features in this irregular length pattern involves the reduced vowel, called *schwa* (/ə/). Because nearly all vowel sounds are reduced to this very short vowel in certain environments, it is the most common sound in the language.

Although *record* (the verb) and *record* (the noun) look alike to a student, in fact the stress patterns are different. Therefore the rhythm of the words (the relative length of the syllables) is patterned differently.

Examples:

1. The first vowel is schwa in *atomic* or *record* (the verb).
2. The second vowel is schwa in *atom* or *record* (the noun).

In English, if the rhythm is so wrong that the listener cannot identify the pattern of stressed and unstressed syllables, the sentence may be unintelligible. This is because English speakers appear to store vocabulary with stress patterns, so a stress mistake can throw a conversation off track, especially if the speaker's control of English vowel sounds is uncertain. As Brown (1977) has pointed out, "From the point of view of the comprehension of spoken English, the ability to identify stressed syllables and make intelligent guesses about the content of the message from this information is absolutely essential" (p. 91).

Examples:

1. That's elementary / a lemon tree.
2. We're interested in history / his story.
3. What do you think of this comedy / committee?

Gadget: Rubber bands. The teaching point is that in English some syllables are longer than others: "From the point of view of teaching perception and production of rhythm, length is the variable that most students find easiest to control, and it is a reliable marker of stress" (Brown, 1990, p. 46). And, as Wong has noted, "The heart of the rhythmic system—syllable length—may be initially difficult for students to apprehend through the ear but may be more clearly demonstrated through the use of the other senses" (1987, p. 25).

To overcome the tendency to use the rhythmic structure of the L1, teachers can demonstrate variable length by saying a word while pulling a wide rubber band between their two thumbs. Stretching it out during the stressed syllable but leaving it short during other syllables provides a visual image of the variable length of the syllables. If the students receive similar bands to use while they practice speaking, they can have a kinesthetic tool that mimics the actual effort involved in lengthening a stressed syllable. (Note: A narrow rubber band is apt to break and does not convey the real mental effort involved.)

Minilesson. Say these words, stretching the rubber band for the stressed syllable.

Examples:

sofa	open	around	allow	Alaska	Canada
--	-- .	. ---	. ---	. --	-- . .

Sentence Rhythm

As Morley (1979) has noted, "Sentence stresses are the strong parts in the rhythm of the sentence. The speaker gives more strength to certain parts to help the listener get the sense (or the meaning) of the sentence" (p. 38).

Minilesson. Lengthen the stressed syllables of the most important words.

Examples:
1. X: I want some SHOES.
   Y: What KIND of shoes?
   X: CAsual shoes. (Gilbert, 1984, p. 38)
2. A: What did you have for starters?
   B: I had chicken soup.
   A: What did the others have?
   B: Chris had tomato soup and James had tomato salad. (Bradford, 1988, p. 8)

Melody

Change in pitch appears to be one of the most significant features in identifying sentence accents (the most-stressed word in the sentence): "Though it is wrong to identify accent with any of its various cues, there are reasons for believing that pitch is the one most heavily relied on" (Bolinger, 1986, p. 21).

L2 learners have difficulty hearing intonation. When they listen to speech, they are powerfully distracted from attending to pitch changes because they are struggling to understand sounds, vocabulary, and grammar. Many learners also seem to have a tendency to speak in a monotone either because of nervous tension or simply because they are concentrating their conscious attention on grammar and vocabulary. Thus learning to attend to melody can help both speaking and listening.

Gadget: Kazoos. How can teachers do a better job of helping students pay attention to the pitch patterns of English? One way is to offer them a speech model stripped of everything but melody, allowing them to concentrate on that specific aspect of English. A cheap and entertaining technique to do this is to use a toy kazoo, which amplifies the vibration of the vocal cords. By humming into it, the teacher can give a sharp demonstration of the intonation of a sentence. (Plastic kazoos can be bought cheaply by the gross at party goods shops.) Students are always startled and amused when the kazoo is first introduced, but once their attention is caught, they learn to see it as a helpful aid for intensifying concentration.

Minilesson. Learning to guess the implications of emphasis is a great aid to listening comprehension.

Examples: Choice of answers

The first student chooses to say (or kazoo) either (a) or (b). The second student must answer with words appropriate to this choice.

1. a. It's a big DOG.
   Answer: No, it's a wolf.
   b. It's a BIG dog.
   Answer: More medium sized.
2. a. But we asked for two COKES!
   Answer: Oh, I thought you wanted tea.
   b. But we asked for TWO Cokes!
   Answer: Oh, I thought you wanted one.
3. a. We prefer beef SOUP.
   Answer: Not stew?
   b. We prefer BEEF soup.
   Answer: Not chicken? (Gilbert, 1993, p. 90)

The Purpose of Intonation: Helping the Listener to Follow

English Emphasis

[We] need to treat intonation not as a function of grammar or attitude, but primarily as a function of discourse, with implications for context and for moment by moment assessment of the communicative value of each part of each utterance. (Brazil et al., 1980, p. 128)

Emphasis and pause act as the navigational guides by which the speaker helps the listener to follow. These discourse signals keep the conversation on track. The simplest way to explain the function of sentence emphasis is in terms of *old information*, which refers to ideas already discussed or mutually understood, and *new information*, a thought to which the speaker wishes to call special attention. Every language has a way to show this difference. For instance, Japanese uses a particle ending, and German uses the signal word *doch*. In English, intonation is the main way to show the special importance of particular words. The system works by contrast: emphasis and deemphasis. Words whose referents are old information are pronounced with relatively weaker stress and lower pitch. Words that are the focus of thought, the new information, are highlighted by intonation—a lengthening of the stressed syllable and a change in the pitch: "Highlighting, by means of the application of a pitch-stress focus . . . is very frequently used to emphasize an item the speaker thinks is particularly important, or that carries new and contrasting information" (Bowen, 1975, p. 91).

Example:
Did you have a good day?
Answer: I had a bloody HORRible day. (Cruttendon, 1986, p. 89)

Native speakers of English generally assume that this intonational emphasis is a natural part of speech, but in fact it is highly language specific. Therefore, when learners speak in a monotone and are also ignorant of syllable lengthening, the crucial contrast is lost.

Allen (1971) gives some exceptionally clear examples of shifting focus of attention:

A: I've lost an umBRELLa.
B: A LAdy's umbrella?
A: Yes. A lady's umbrella with STARS on it. GREEN stars. (p. 77)

Minilesson.

Examples:

For the following activity Student A chooses to say one of the sentences in the pair. Student B must answer according to the emphasis heard.

A: WERE you in the bank on Friday?
B: No, I wasn't.

A: Were YOU in the bank on Friday?
B: No, but my SISTER was.

A: Were you IN the bank on Friday?
B: No, but I was NEAR it. (Rogerson & Gilbert, 1990, p. 49)

For the following activity B uses the same words to respond to the two different things that A says. The challenge is to decide which of A's remarks was implied by B's response (depending on which word B chooses to emphasize).

A: Paul looks happy!
A: I think Paul needs a new car.
B: He's got a new car.

A: We must get some flowers.
A: Don't forget to get them a present.
B: I've got some flowers. (Bradford, 1988, p. 9)

The Learner's Own Words

How can teachers help students acquire intonational emphasis as part of their natural use of English outside the classroom?

> Learners need to be made aware of the communicative value of intonation rather than merely of its physical characteristics. They then need to be given a chance to use intonation interactively, and not to simply repeat it. (Pirt, 1990, p. 155)

Minilesson.

Examples:

1. Prediction: What might be said next? Complete the following sentence, taking into account the implication of the emphasis.
   My SISTER got a raise but _____. (Mendelsohn, 1992)
2. Write responses to the following remarks. More than one answer is possible. Underline the word in your answer that contradicts the remark.
   Example:
   A: London is far away.
   B: No, it's *near*. (or) Not *very* far. (or) Not as far as *Rome*.
   a. A: Paris and London are countries.
      B:
   b. A: You buy books in libraries.
      B:
   c. A: People are sad when they receive good news from home.
      B:
3. Orientation: What might have been said before? Guessing what was said before is especially important if the previous remark was not heard clearly. Write a remark by A that would cause B to answer with emphasis on the capitalized word.
   Example:
   A: Today is Monday.
   B: No, today is TUESDAY.
   a. A:
      B: No, the wedding is on the FIFTH of April.
   b. A:
      B: I don't agree. We need MORE rain.
   c. A:
      B: In MY opinion, the music is VERY good.

After this kind of semicontrolled work, students should be given small-group discussion tasks that naturally call for contrastive stress. An example of this kind of activity is to ask students to compare and contrast the business customs of their countries in such areas as business cards, handshakes, gift giving, length of a typical work day, and so on (Grant, 1993, p. 128).

Thought Groups

English speakers help their listeners to follow not only by using contrastive emphasis but by combining words into thought groups so that ideas can be more easily processed. Usually each thought group has one focus word.

Examples (of relatively short groupings):

1. The sign says that CONSTRUCTION / will be finished by APRIL, / but that was obviously OPTIMISTIC.
2. Even when I was a KID, / I knew that the IN crowd / was just SHOW / and OTHER people / were really more INTERESTING.

Falling pitches and pauses mark the end of thought groups. Pauses give the listener time to think about what was just said. This processing time is especially important if pronunciation or grammatical sources of confusion are present. Learners who fail to notice signals of emphasis and thought grouping miss important information.

Minilesson.

Examples:

For this activity say the following pairs aloud and notice how the punctuation is indicated in the spoken language:

a. John said, "The Boss is crazy."
   (Who is speaking?)
b. "John," said the Boss, "is crazy."
   (Who is speaking?)

a. (2 + 3) x 4 = 20
b. 2 + (3 x 4) = 14

For the following activity Student 1 chooses to say (a) or (b), separating the items by using a falling pitch or a pause. Student 2 answers the question according to the sentence heard.

a. He sold his house, boat, and trailer.
   (How many things did he sell?)
b. He sold his houseboat and trailer.
   (How many things did he sell?)

a. She likes pie and apples.
   (What does she like?)
b. She likes pineapples.
   (What does she like?) (Gilbert, 1993, p. 113)

To improve clarity of both speech and listening, students need to learn to use pauses and pitch falls to mark groups. A simple way to begin is with the dictation of telephone numbers. If the numbers are not grouped correctly, the listener has difficulty processing the number, even if the individual parts are pronounced well.

Pairs or small groups can mark dialogues for thought groups. The important thing is not *where* the students divide the group but that they think about the need to help their listener to follow.

Summary

By teaching linking, rhythm, stress and intonation, teachers can place pronunciation teaching within a communicative setting. By using a variety of practical kinesthetic, visual, and aural teaching devices, they can help students sharpen their ability to attend to key features of spoken English.

Note

1. An earlier version of this chapter appeared in the August 1992 issue of *Speak Out!*, the newsletter of the International Association of Teaching English as a Foreign Language Pronunciation Special Interest Group.

References

Abberton, E., Parker, A., & Fourcin, A. (1978). Speech improvements in deaf adults using laryngograph displays. In *Speech and hearing work in progress* (pp. 33–60). University College of London, Department of Phonetics and Linguistics.

Allen, V. F. (1971). Teaching intonation, from theory to practice. *TESOL Quarterly*, 4, 73–91.

Bolinger, D. L. (1986). *Intonation and its parts*. Palo Alto, CA: Stanford University Press.

Bowen, J. D. (1975). *Patterns of English pronunciation*. Rowley, MA: Newbury House.

Bradford, B. (1988). *Intonation in context*. Cambridge: Cambridge University Press.

Brazil, D., Coulthard, M., & Johns, C. (1980). *Discourse intonation and language teaching*. London: Longman.

Brown, A. (Ed.) (1991). *Teaching English pronunciation: A book of readings*. London: Routledge.

Brown, G. (1977). *Listening to spoken English*. London: Longman.

Brown, G. (1990). *Listening to spoken English* (2nd ed.). London: Longman.

Cruttendon, A. (1986). *Intonation*. Cambridge: Cambridge University Press.

Forster, E. M. (1951). *A passage to India*. New York: Harcourt Brace Jovanovich. (Original work published 1924)

Gilbert, J. B. (1984). *Clear speech: Pronunciation and listening comprehension in American English.* New York: Cambridge University Press.

Gilbert, J. B. (1993). *Clear speech: Pronunciation and listening comprehension in North American English* (2nd ed.). New York: Cambridge University Press.

Grant, L. (1993). *Well said: Advanced English pronunciation.* Boston: Heinle & Heinle.

Mendelsohn, D. (1992, March). *Strategies for listening comprehension.* Plenary speech given at the 26th Annual TESOL Convention, Vancouver, BC.

Morley, J. (1979). *Improving spoken English.* Ann Arbor: University of Michigan Press.

Pirt, G. (1990). Discourse intonation problems for non-native speakers. In M. Hewings (Ed.), *Papers in discourse intonation.* Birmingham, England: University of Birmingham.

Rogerson, P., & Gilbert, J. (1990). *Speaking clearly.* Cambridge: Cambridge University Press.

Wong, R. (1987). *Teaching pronunciation.* Englewood Cliffs, NJ: Prentice-Hall.

— 4 —
Some Perspectives on Accent: Range of Voice Quality Variation, the Periphery, and Focusing

John H. Esling
University of Victoria

Editorial Notes

John Esling focuses on some critical features of speech production and speech perception and the significant roles they play in L2 accent analysis and modification as well as L1 dialect studies. He describes two levels of speech analysis. The first—well known to L2 teachers—involves the *segmental phonemes* of a given language; this narrow segmental dimension of speech production comprises the discrete sound units of a given language or dialect. The second level—well known to phoneticians and phonologists but perhaps not so familiar to L2 teachers—involves the broader dimension of voice quality settings; this dimension focuses on the *long-term articulatory postures* of speech production and the set of global properties of a language or dialect. In relating the behaviors of these two dimensions, that is, the interaction of the segmentals in an accent to the global voice quality features, Esling explores the implications for pedagogical procedures in L2 speech and pronunciation.

Esling presents a descriptive taxonomy for the range of voice quality settings and succinct, informative descriptions and definitions. Descriptive phonetic labels for voice quality settings are presented in two groups. The first, *laryngeal settings* or phonation types, describes the wide range of phonatory qualities that the human vocal mechanism can produce. The second group, *supralaryngeal settings*, describes the muscular postures of the vocal tract above the larynx. The vocal characteristics achieved by a raising or a lowering of the larynx are discussed first, followed by a variety of features involving articulations of the lips, jaw, and tongue. These include the modifications of labiodentalization (i.e., "overbite" style), jaw protrusion, jaw-closed and jaw-open posturing, lip rounding (i.e., pursing) or spreading, and nasality-denasality. Esling points out that the interaction of these long-term vocal settings with the short-term segmental phoneme elements needs to be made more precise in second language acquisition theory.

Next Esling reviews recent research on *voice quality*. First he examines *auditory modeling*, a research approach that has yielded a growing base of data on prototypical examples of settings, probing to the periphery of all possible vocal settings and how they behave relative to segmental units. He notes that, just as phonologies of languages differ, so must the long-term prosodic features on which those phonological inventories are built. Further, he postulates that L2 learners may very well begin to recognize these traits *before* they are able to isolate single phonemic units in the phonology. Esling then turns to a discussion of syllabic features, looking at an area of research that originates in the perceptual study of consonant-vowel sequences. This research indicates that a segmental explanation of how a phonology is acquired is probably incomplete. A variety of research data on this aspect of phonology is presented.

Finally, Esling examines research relating to *voice quality settings in social context*, which suggests that sociolinguistically distinct groups retain that distinction by means of the broader dimensions of long-term habitual vocal-setting postures. Moreover, these underlying articulatory posture indicators mirror somewhat the differences in the narrower, discrete-unit dimension of segmental phonology, although not completely.

In concluding, Esling observes that voice quality settings may help L1 speakers and L2 learners to gain some degree of control over a number of segmental features simultaneously.

J.M.

Some Perspectives on Accent: Range of Voice Quality Variation, the Periphery, and Focusing

In phonetics and phonology the speech patterns of a language are analyzed on at least two levels: (a) the narrower segmental dimension and (b) the broader voice quality settings dimension (also termed *long-term articulatory postures*).

The first level focuses on discrete units of linguistic meaning—the chain of segmental phonemes of a language. The second level focuses on global properties—features that do not necessarily have linguistic meaning but that those phonemes have in common. In the next section I review the descriptive labels used for talking about voice quality. I then present some of the research that indicates the importance of global properties of accent. Finally, I focus on relating the behavior of the segmental phonemes in an accent to the global background vocal-setting features, as explored in recent sociolinguistic research.

The information and instructional applications presented in this paper, though based on exploratory research data, have a significant potential value for L2 pronunciation pedagogy. Phoneticians with an interest in L2 learning and teaching have known for a long time that individuals can imitate and selectively modify voice quality settings—long-term articulatory postures—to effect a global change in their accent, often resulting in a more authentic impression of a target language accent (Abercrombie, 1967; Honikman, 1964). For readers familiar with this literature, the enumeration of voice quality setting features is not new; it is a familiar taxonomy already used to describe L2 students' accents as well as the accents of L1 native speakers whom L2 student learners might regard as models. Taken a step further, application of vocal-setting information to L2 pronunciation instruction in the form of conscious, explicit tutelage in the production of a range of setting features may be a useful direction to explore. However, that approach should not be interpreted as a proven method of shaping student accents in the L2. Its success would depend on a number of factors, including

- the relationship between explicit learning and eventual acquisition
- contexts of exposure and observation
- the salience of individual models for a given learner
- individual learners' personalities and predispositions
- dramatic ability.

So, although the successful application of descriptive knowledge to pedagogical procedures is far from straightforward, a number of research developments in the identification of voice quality features and their possible role in the perception of accent are of interest to report.

The Range of Voice Quality Settings in Accent

This section will discuss terminology and explain the descriptive taxonomy for the voice quality settings that are used in this paper as a basis for talking about accent.

Laryngeal Settings: Phonation Types

The first part of Table 1 presents the range of types of phonation that a speaker may demonstrate as a product of how the vocal cords, or vocal folds, are vibrating. Some of these labels refer to states of the glottis (the opening in the laryngeal "valve" that connects the trachea and the pharynx). These types of phonation involve no voicing but feature only the restricted passage of air, or a combination of some type of voicing along with the restricted passage of air. *Whisper*, for example, is produced by narrowing the channel at the glottis to generate only a little more friction (fricative noise) than does breath ("breathing through the mouth") as in a quiet sigh. Interestingly, the research into the acoustic differences between settings indicates that whisper is the most distinct of the phonation types in terms of a speaker's production (Harmegnies, Esling, & Delplancq, 1989). That is, the long-term acoustic properties of whisper differ the most from a speaker's other phonation types. This finding suggests that listeners may perceive whisper differently, although further testing is required to establish this, and that whisper may be the most effective mode of phonation that a speaker could adopt to disguise his or her voice. Whisper is, after all, used paralinguistically as the register of secrecy. In studying second language acquisition (SLA), it may be worth observing where and when learners have a chance to use whisper and whether practicing whispering has an effect on how they view their accent in the target language. In a teaching task, whispered speech would be predicted to give the learner the widest variation from his or her voiced speech while

Table 1
Descriptive Phonetic Labels for Voice Quality Settings

Laryngeal settings (phonation types)			
Simple	*Compound*		
Whisper			
Creak	Whispery creak	Harsh creak	
Modal voice	Whispery voice	Creaky voice	Harsh voice
	Harsh whispery voice	Harsh creaky voice	
	Whispery creaky voice	Harsh whispery creaky voice	
Falsetto	Whispery falsetto	Creaky falsetto	Harsh falsetto
	Harsh whispery falsetto	Harsh creaky falsetto	
	Whispery creaky falsetto	Harsh whispery creaky falsetto	
	Breathy voice	Ventricular voice	

Supralaryngeal settings		
Neutral setting		
Raised larynx	Labiodentalized	
Lowered larynx	Protruded jaw	Spread lips
	Close jaw	Close rounding
	Open jaw	Open rounding
	Dentalized	
Tongue tip articulation	Alveolarized	
Tongue blade articulation	Palato-alveolarized	
Retroflex articulation	Palatalized	
	Velarized	Nasal
	Uvularized	Denasal
	Pharyngealized	
	Laryngo-pharyngealized	Faucalized

Note. Adapted from Esling (1994).

exploiting the periphery of modes of voice production in a "most disguised" and presumably safer environment.

Creak, modal (or *neutral*) *voice*, and *falsetto* can be said to represent the *pitch range from lowest to highest*. Most people can produce, or imitate, creak or a creaky voice by saying a sustained [ɑ] vowel on their lowest "note"—as low in their pitch range as they can go. Falsetto, on the other hand, exploits the high end of the range of possible variation in the chosen medium. It is often used in singing, for effect (e.g., Frankie Valli, the Bee Gees) or perhaps for the sake of contrast. In puppet theatre, Frank Oz of the Muppets uses falsetto as Miss Piggy—in contrast to other characters that require a lower register.

Beyond pitch, phonation types can be characterized primarily by the degree of *whisperiness, creakiness,* or *harshness* that is present. Whisperiness and creakiness are more highly valued (in the sense of sociolinguistic prestige) in some varieties of British English, whereas harshness functions as an indicator of some varieties of dialectal speech (Laver & Trudgill, 1979, p. 15). Harshness can also be highly valued as in many popular singing styles, including the Italian popular tradition, British rock music, and U.S. country music. The two opposites at the bottom of the list—*breathy voice* and *ventricular voice*—represent the most open and the most constricted glottal configurations, respectively. Whereas whispery voice describes the louder "stage whisper" (to give the impression of a whisper while adding voice for efficient projection), breathy voice is quiet, associated impressionistically with "sexy" voice as in the singing of Julio Iglesias (see Catford, 1964, and Laver, 1980, for technical explanations of these degrees of glottal openness). Ventricular voice accompanies heavy lifting—straining, as in weight lifting—wherever the laryngeal valve needs to be almost closed for efficient respiratory muscular apposition. It is the last phonatory stage before a "massive" glottal stop, in which the airway is closed and the larynx is covered up.

Supralaryngeal Settings: The Range of Articulatory Settings

The bottom panel of Table 1 presents the range of articulatory settings or muscular postures of the vocal tract above the larynx (i.e., supralaryngeal settings). Each is viewed as a single departure from the idealized neutral setting. *Raised larynx* and *faucalized voice* share some common traits of place of articulation and, in effect, join the two opposite ends of the chart full circle. The best-known Jim Hensen Muppet alter-voice is achieved largely by raising the larynx, although faucalization is added intermittently for contrast and perhaps pitch control. This is the effect often achieved in shouting over a distance, when *not* using a high-pitched (falsetto) style. It is the quality referred to impressionistically by Bell as the "cry of a peacock" in early descriptions of some hearing-impaired speech (see Laver, 1980). Lowering of the larynx may very well accompany faucalization when the pitch of the voice appears to remain high. Otherwise, *lowered larynx voice* usually implies an association with low-pitched voicing. In North America it is a common voice for serious occasions, at least in northern U.S. and central Canadian dialects—public-address announcements, political speeches, or radio news.

Supralaryngeal Settings: Articulations of the Lips, Jaw, and Tongue

The bottom panel of Table 1 represents articulations of the lips, jaw, and tongue, moving progressively farther back in the mouth reading down the list. The three settings of the front of the tongue (to the left) are elaborations of or modifications to the four most-fronted tongue-body postures (to their right). A *labiodentalized* configuration refers to an overbite style, where the upper teeth cover the lower lip. Many southern English accents, such as Cockney, have this visually recognizable style. Shifts in consonant values, as in Cockney, in which [θ] varies as [f] and [ð] varies as [v], can be captured economically by citing the superimposed setting as a prosodic, global trait. The London accent contrasts with an Edinburgh accent in that the latter exemplifies *protruded jaw*—the lower lip is prominent. A *close-jaw* setting, almost clenching the teeth, characterizes British English accents better than many U.S. accents, which often have a more *open-jaw* posture. Note that dialect regions often differ, as in a "closed-mouthed" Massachusetts style described by Labov (1972, p. 40), but this simply illustrates the range of variation to which language learners are exposed and of which they must be aware (to the extent that the phonology to be acquired is economically represented by global setting features).

Settings of the body of the tongue have a dramatic effect on a series of consonants in the phonology. The most fronted, *dentalized* setting of the tongue is more common on the west coast of North America, while so-called General American can usually be characterized as *alveolarized* or *palato-alveolarized*. Baby talk in English is often *palatalized* (if lip-rounded as well) as if emulating a small vocal tract. The effect on consonants can be pervasive—adding a [j] off-glide throughout. Lancashire accents are often used as examples of *velarized* articulation, and Yorkshire often illustrates *uvularization*, although these divisions are by no means so clear-cut regionally. The same tongue backing found as a secondary articulation in the north of England is also found in accents of the southern United States—for example, in many Black Vernacular English accents. *Pharyngealization* is the more extreme tongue backing sometimes used prosodically to describe Arabic; and a *laryngo-pharyngealized* setting is the most retracted tongue setting, found in some working-class accents of western Canada.

Spread lips can be distinguished easily over the telephone (when the speaker is smiling) whereas *close rounding* (almost pursing) of the lips has the same effect on the acoustic spectrum of speech as blowing across the mouth of an empty bottle. Smiling shortens the vocal tract, paralleling a short wind instrument (the flute) whereas the longer vocal tract produced by protruding the lips parallels a longer one (the bassoon). *Open rounding* resembles the sustained quality of an [œ] vowel, which could be used to characterize several Scandinavian accents.

Finally, constant or intermittent *nasality* is found in many accents—of American English, British English, French, and Brazilian Portuguese, to name just a few—and it is sometimes a highly valued trait and in other circumstances a less prestigious social marker. In speech pathology, its extreme incidence is termed *hypernasality*. *Denasal voice* describes the "cold-in-the-nose" effect and is termed *hyponasality* in speech pathology.

The chance to notice, remember, and learn particular voice quality settings as they occur in sociolinguistic contexts depends on the L2 learner's exposure to situations in which speakers who are similar in some respect display details of voice quality that are similar. Categorizing voice quality types as they vary systematically within the range of settings present in the target language can be a useful learning exercise. This hypothesis implies that students are searching for a setting or combination of settings that they will feel comfortable adopting in their new language (L2), although to different degrees and within different critical windows.[1] This phenomenon relates to the "focusing" principle, referred to in Esling (1990), whereby the sampling that a learner exercises in practising new aspects of the L2 exceeds what would be judged as correct (cf. overlearning) before finally returning to the narrower range increasingly identified as the target value for that aspect of the learner's phonetic performance. One relationship that needs to be made more precise in SLA theory is the interaction of the long-term level of vocal setting with the short-term segmental phoneme elements of a phonology.

Research Relating to Voice Quality

Auditory Modeling

One research approach that has provided a growing base of data on settings and how they behave relative to segmental units is the acoustic analysis of auditorily specified models. These models represent prototypical examples of each setting in an attempt to probe to the periphery of all possible vocal quality settings—long-term articulatory adjustments. In theory, then, each prototypical production of a setting aims to define the most extreme effect that setting will have on a series of consonants and vowels. Such a theoretical perspective implies a parallel with the process that language learners encounter when they begin to be exposed to the different voices of the different

Figure 1
Long-Term Average Spectra: Velarized Versus Palatalized Voice

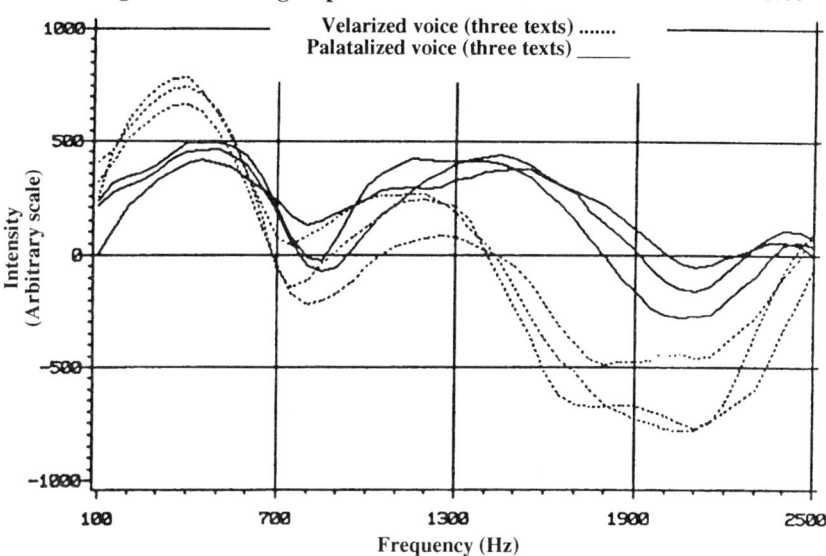

accents of the L2. As phonologies differ, so must the long-term, prosodic features on which those phonological inventories are built. It is therefore reasonable to hypothesize that learners perceive and begin to recognize long-term traits *before* they are able to isolate single systematic units in the phonology (phonemes). Here, too, much more research is needed to establish the validity of such a "general-to-specific" process of accent acquisition or to explain how it works. Nevertheless, a few sets of teaching materials for listening and speaking already emphasize the importance of prosody before moving on to segmental detail (Gilbert, 1984; Dauer, 1993; Morley, 1979).

Some of the long-term vocal-setting acoustic differences that separate the models can be illustrated using long-term average spectral charts of controlled productions by a phonetician. A habitually *nasalized* setting, for example, changes the average distribution of spectral energy so that the concentrations or peaks of energy are in different locations from, say, a palatalized setting without nasalization. Habitual *tongue backing*, as in *velarization* or *laryngopharyngealization*, redistributes the peaks in a direction that resembles the spectral (or formant) peaks of a backed vowel. This comparison between a lingually fronted setting and a backed setting is shown in Figure 1, where each of three phonetic texts of at least 30 seconds in length was articulated with either a palatalized or a velarized setting.

Faucalization contrasts with nasalization in the relative prominence and location of the first versus the second spectral peak. This comparison is

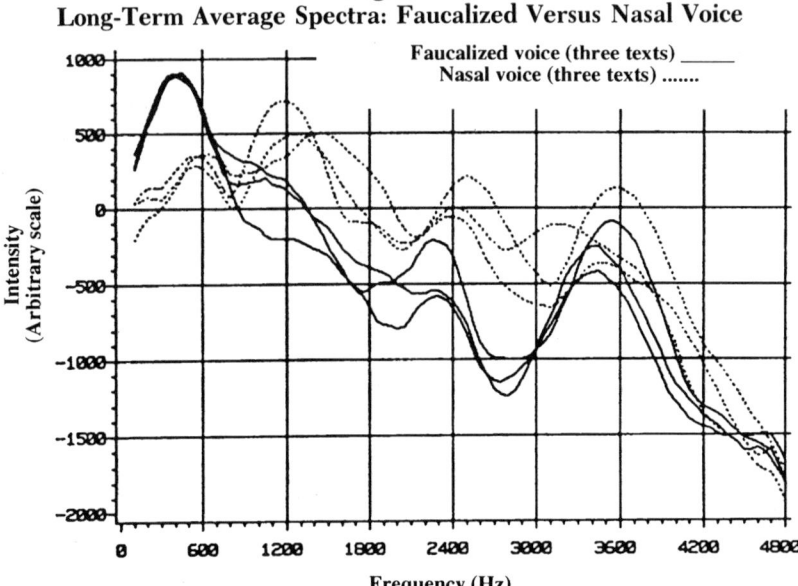

Figure 2
Long-Term Average Spectra: Faucalized Versus Nasal Voice

shown in Figure 2. A considerable amount of work has been done to refine the technique of comparing long-term voice quality spectral averages of speech in different languages, especially using bilingual speakers to control for individual variability (see Bruyninckx, Harmegnies, Llisterri, & Poch-Olivé, 1994; Harmegnies, 1988; Harmegnies & Landercy, 1985). Results are beginning to show that long-term voice quality spectra differ systematically according to the language a speaker is using and that these can be identified articulatorily using models such as those shown in Figures 1 and 2. In the case of French-Flemish bilinguals or Catalan-Castilian bilinguals, for instance, the isolation of register-specific acoustic patterns implies that speakers modify their accents when switching languages by adopting a generalized shift in voice quality setting.

Syllabic Features

Another vein of research indicating that a segmental explanation of how a phonology is acquired is probably incomplete originates in the perceptual study of consonant-vowel (CV) sequences. CV sequences have already been identified as a preferred unit in the interlanguage of L2 acquirers (Tarone, 1978). Traditional contrastive analysis, on the other hand, implies that learners are able to distinguish phonemes for what they are, almost immediately, with no intermediate prosodic step in the process. Recent research indicates that the cues for perceiving what is thought of as a phoneme may not even be present in the given segment, but rather in a neighboring segment in the same syllable.

In a perceptual study of Korean, in which three contrasting manners of articulation distinguish the plosive series, initial plosives in a CV sequence were separated from their following vowel using an instrumental editing technique in the Computerized Speech Lab environment (Esling, 1988). The three manners, often known as *aspirated, lenis*, and *fortis*, are all voiceless but involve progressively shorter amounts of aspiration, or voice onset time (VOT), before voicing begins on the following vowel. The quality of voicing when it occurs on the vowel, however, is not the same for the three manners. When the consonant and aspiration time of the syllable are both removed and only the vowel portion is played back to a Korean listener, recognition of the manner of articulation of the missing plosive remains high, especially in the fortis and lenis cases. Removing the C of the CV sequence still predictably confounds the listener when it comes to identifying the correct place of articulation of the missing C, but the critical difference in manner of articulation characteristic of Korean is preserved in the vowel alone—even in the absence of aspiration or timing cues. Further tests in which Cs and Vs from different syllables are combined in all possible permutations confirm that, whereas long VOT generally signals the aspirated manner of articulation, vowel quality is more important than VOT in influencing the listener's perception of fortis and lenis consonants.

An even more striking result of follow-up research is that the acoustic cues that apparently signal which type of syllable is being spoken behave differently for different vowels (Esling, 1991a). Characteristics of the detail of vocal-fold closing and opening can be compared using a technique of analysis in which the periods of vibration of the vocal folds are measured directly rather than through the speech signal. The resulting laryngographic, or so-called *Lx*, waveforms yield a lower closing-to-opening ratio for more laryngealized phonation types and a higher closing-to-opening ratio for whisperier and breathier phonation types. This relationship can be seen graphically in Figure 3, where the three manners of articulation demonstrate distinct patterns of Lx waveform behaviour. The fortis CVs are the most laryngealized, and the aspirated CVs appear to have the highest ratio of openness during vocalic voicing. The pattern differs, however, according to what vowel is in the syllable. On the most open vowel in the Korean vowel system, /ɑ/, the lenis CV sequences demonstrate most whispery or breathy behavior. So a prosodic phenomenon (of phonation type) initially presumed to apply uniformly wherever vocalic voicing occurs is found to apply differentially. Although most vowels follow the expected pattern of how they are to be voiced, one vowel departs sharply from that pattern. Phonological variabil-

Figure 3
Vowels Following Stops and s- in Korean; Mean Lx Ratios by Vowel Category

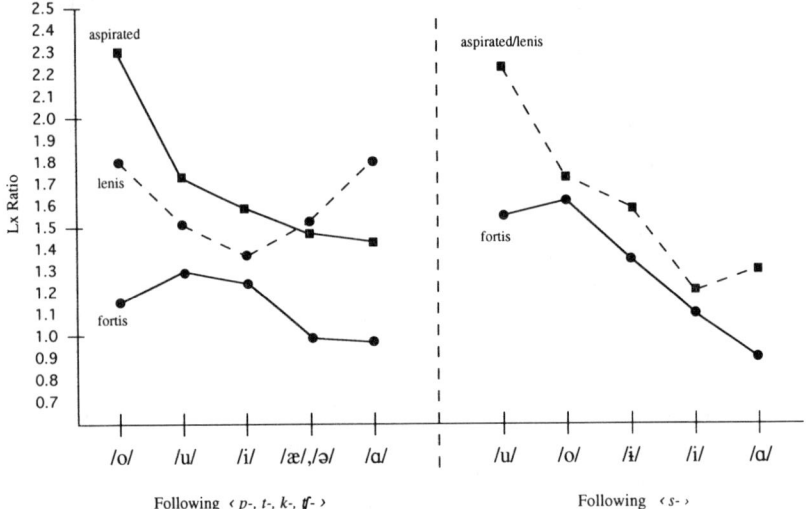

ity has of course been identified in sociolinguistics as a mechanism of language change and as a reflection of the most inherent characteristic of language— that it varies. What is new here is that the range of variation depends to some extent on the limits imposed on the shorter-term fluctuations of consonants and vowels by the background of longer-term articulatory phenomena. This view is reinforced by recent investigations into the sociolinguistic distribution of voice quality settings.

Voice Quality Settings in Social Context

Research has shown that speakers vary in the voice quality settings of their accents according to the social dialect they speak. The social differentiation of English in Vancouver is marked by a shift in voice quality from more retracted settings in working-class speech to more fronted and/or nasal settings in middle-class speech (Esling, 1991b; Esling, in press). Without any explicit tutelage, speakers are presumably aware of these differences in a global sense (to the extent that a given individual is at all sensitive to differences in accent). Native speakers appear to be able to effect a remarkable coordination of their vocal production so that they can match each others' vocal settings so closely. It would therefore seem entirely reasonable for L2 teachers to expect many if not most L2 acquirers to be sensitive to features of voice quality settings and for teachers to exploit this sensitivity by preparing teaching units that present and explore the range of settings ("voices") found in the target language. Suggestions for such a methodology were initiated in Esling and Wong (1983) and elaborated in Esling (1987). They included a listening exercise that challenges learners to recognize the age, sex, regional origin, educational background, and occupational history of a tape-recorded speaker, based solely on auditory cues.

Even more significant in this research on social dialects is that the shifts in vocal setting from group to group, originally thought to apply uniformly to all segmental elements of the phonology, appear to apply variably depending on the vowel in question (Esling & Warkentyne, 1993; Warkentyne & Esling, in press). This finding corresponds to those of the laryngographic studies mentioned above, which indicated that phonologically specified CV series vary in the pattern of phonation used depending on the vocalic environment. A generalized fronting of most vowels among Vancouver women with highest social status, for instance, is a trend not shared by the /æ/ vowel, which appears to be retracting. Retraction of /æ/ among younger speakers of Canadian English is in direct contrast with the fronting and raising of this vowel reported in the northern United States. This reverse-trend phenomenon means that one or two or three vowels in a phonological system may be acting as pivots, sliding against a trend that would otherwise be uniform.

This research suggests that sociolinguistically distinct groups maintain their regional or social identities by means of the long-term, habitual, articulatory postures of accent that are described as *voice quality settings* (i.e., the broader dimension). These long-term articulatory posture indicators or markers reflect to some degree the differences in *segmental phonology* (i.e., the narrower discrete-unit dimension) between the contrasting groups, *but the two levels of accent are not parallel at all points*. As in the studies of Vancouver English vowels, most vowels shift in a uniform direction that parallels the long-term voice quality spectral properties of the voices representing that group. Some vowels, on the other hand, appear to defy the generalized pattern, pulling one part of the vowel system in a new and different direction.

These detailed relationships between the levels of accent suggest that long-term voice quality settings are a potentially valuable mechanism for speakers to use in effecting slight but significant control over a number of segmental features at the same time. Some segmental pronunciations may stand out as clear exceptions to this "configurational norm," but such variation is to be expected in language use and language change.

A Final Note

The mechanism of the prototypical role of vocal quality is also available to L2 learners. What is required is an approach that explores the rich body of data provided by the relatively sudden encounter of language learners with the distribution of voice quality settings found in the target language. How learners adapt to these encounters with differentiation in accent may reveal a considerable amount not only about the processes of exploring the periphery of available input and of focusing on one's own accent as an L2 speaker, but also about the long-term mechanisms that mediate the ongoing process of phonological change internal to the target language.

Note

1. Editor's note: Observing his awareness of this phenomenon, one of my graduate students once observed, "It feels like I have an English-speaking face and a Chinese-speaking face—and they even look different on the video!"—J.M.

Acknowledgment

The sociophonetic analysis of voice quality in the survey of Vancouver English was made possible by research grants #410-87-0334 and 410-89-0191 from the Social Sciences and Humanities Research Council of Canada.

References

Abercrombie, D. (1967). *Elements of general phonetics*. Edinburgh: Edinburgh University Press.

Bruyninckx, M., Harmegnies, B., Llisterri, J., & Poch-Olivé, D. (1994). Language-induced voice quality variability in bilinguals. *Journal of Phonetics, 22*, 19–31.

Catford, J. C. (1964). Phonation types: The classification of some laryngeal components of speech production. In D. Abercrombie et al. (Eds.), *In honour of Daniel Jones* (pp. 26–37). London: Longman.

Dauer, R. (1993). *Accurate English*. Englewood Cliffs, NJ: Regents/Prentice-Hall.

Esling, J. H. (1987). Methodology for voice setting awareness in language classes. *Revue de Phonétique Appliquée, 85*, 449–473.

Esling, J. H. (1988). Phonetic analysis of Korean obstruents. *Working Papers of the Linguistics Circle of the University of Victoria, 7*, 1–7.

Esling, J. H. (1990). La parole sur ordinateur dans l'enseignement de la phonétique et de la langue seconde: Matière académique au niveau avancé. *Revue de Phonétique Appliquée, 95-96-97*, 145–151.

Esling, J. H. (1991a). Laryngographic analysis of phonation in Korean consonant-vowel sequences. *Working Papers of the Linguistics Circle of the University of Victoria, 10*, 105–114.

Esling, J. H. (1991b). Sociophonetic variation in Vancouver. In J. Cheshire (Ed.), *English around the world: Sociolinguistic perspectives* (pp. 123–133). Cambridge: Cambridge University Press.

Esling, J. H. (1994). Voice quality. In R. Asher et al. (Eds.), *The encyclopedia of language and linguistics* (pp. 4950–4953). Oxford: Pergamon Press.

Esling, J. H. (in press). Vowel systems and voice setting in the Survey of Vancouver English. In G. de Wolf (Ed.), *The survey of Vancouver English, 1976-1980: A sociolinguistic study of urban Canadian English*. Kingston, ON: Queen's University, Strathy Language Unit.

Esling, J. H., & Warkentyne, H. J. (1993). Retracting of /æ/ in Vancouver English. In S. Clarke (Ed.), *Focus on Canada* (pp. 229–246). Amsterdam: John Benjamins.

Esling, J. H., & Wong, R. F. (1983). Voice quality settings and the teaching of pronunciation. *TESOL Quarterly, 17*, 89–95. Reprinted in A. Brown (Ed.), 1991, *Teaching English pronunciation* (pp. 288–295). London: Routledge, Chapman & Hall.

Gilbert, J. B. (1984). *Clear speech: Pronunciation and listening comprehension in American English*. Cambridge: Cambridge University Press.

Harmegnies, B. (1988). *Contribution à la caractérisation de la qualité vocale*. Doctoral dissertation, Université de Mons-Hainaut, Mons, Belgium.

Harmegnies, B., Esling, J. H., & Delplancq, V. (1989). Quantitative study of the effects of setting changes on the LTAS. *Eurospeech '89: European Conference on Speech Communication and Technology, 2*, 139–142. Edinburgh: CEP Consultants.

Harmegnies, B., & Landercy, A. (1985). Language features in the long-term average spectrum. *Revue de Phonétique Appliquée, 73-74-75*, 69–79.

Honikman, B. (1964). Articulatory settings. In D. Abercrombie et al. (Eds.), *In honour of Daniel Jones* (pp. 73–84). London: Longman.

Labov, W. (1972). *Sociolinguistic patterns*. Philadelphia: University of Pennsylvania Press.

Laver, J. (1980). *The phonetic description of voice quality*. Cambridge: Cambridge University Press.

Laver, J., & Trudgill, P. (1979). Phonetic and linguistic markers in speech. In K. R. Scherer & H. Giles (Eds.), *Social markers in speech* (pp. 1–32). Cambridge: Cambridge University Press.

Morley, J. (1979). *Improving spoken English: An intensive personalized program in perception, pronunciation, practice in context*. Ann Arbor: University of Michigan Press.

Tarone, E. (1978). The phonology of interlanguage. In J. C. Richards (Ed.), *Understanding second and foreign language learning: Issues and approaches* (pp. 15–33). Rowley, MA: Newbury House.

Warkentyne, H. J., & Esling, J. H. (in press). The low vowels of Vancouver English. In J. Windsor Lewis (Ed.), *Studies in general and English phonetics: Essays in honour of Prof. J. D. O'Connor*. London: Routledge.

— 5 —
A Multidimensional Curriculum Design for Speech-Pronunciation Instruction

Joan Morley
The University of Michigan

Editorial Notes

Joan Morley begins her paper with some background commentary on the recent renewal of interest in pronunciation teaching in ESL and then challenges the wisdom of four conventional notions about pronunciation: that *pronunciation isn't important*, that *students will pick it up on their own*, that *pronunciation can't be taught*, and that *teachers feel they don't know how to teach pronunciation*. She feels that the final concern is valid and is one that can be overcome with renewed efforts in both preservice and inservice training.

The next section discusses two factors involved in the spread of interest in pronunciation programs. The first is a growing concern for learners' problems and unmet learner needs. Nonnative speakers may experience one or more of the following problems: (a) complete breakdown in communication, (b) ineffectual speech performance, (c) negative judgments about personal qualities, (d) anticipatory-apprehensive listener reactions, and (e) pejorative stereotyping. The second factor is the emergence of new directions in instructional design: The principles of pronunciation teaching have been reconceptualized and its pedagogical horizons have expanded. Changes have occurred in (a) program philosophy; (b) learner goals, standards, and outcomes; (c) learning dimensions and teaching objectives; (d) instructional features; (e) the role of the learner; and (f) the role of the teacher.

Morley then presents some views on *expanding the horizons of pronunciation teaching* and discusses changes in both principles and practices. In comparing past and present perspectives on pronunciation, she notes that, although traditional pronunciation teaching procedures appear to have focused primarily, if not exclusively, on linguistic competence (in the terms of Canale & Swain, 1980), today's instructional frameworks are moving toward an expanded concern for three additional areas of communicative competence: *discourse competence, sociolinguistic competence*, and *strategic competence*. Major shifts in the instructional focus of ESL pronunciation programs include (a) attention to communicative principles, (b) a significant focus on suprasegmentals, (c) an expanded domain of what is included under the rubric *pronunciation*, (d) changing perspectives on the roles of the learner and teacher, (e) practice activities aligned along specific-purposes contextualizations, (f) a renewed focus on the reciprocal listening-speaking connection, (g) special attention to sound-spelling relationships, and (h) a focus on individualization and the uniqueness of each learner.

Morley then discusses six aspects of a multidimensional curriculum design. The first sets forth the basic underlying principle: a dual-focus program philosophy. In this conceptualization one focus is on a *micro level*, with attention directed to the discrete elements of pronunciation, and the second focus is on the *macro level*, with attention directed to global elements of communicability in particular settings and a specific goal of developing discourse competence, sociolinguistic competence, and strategic competence in addition to linguistic competence. The other features of instructional planning include a comprehensive set of communicative goals for learners, with attention to competencies and learners' strategies; an integrated approach paradigm of instructional objectives and learner involvement; curriculum guidelines for instructional planning, including assessment procedures, a continuum of instructional components, and specific attention to the development of learning strategies; a revised conceptualization of the learner's role and responsibilities; and a revised conceptualization of the teacher's responsibilities and the role of the teacher as coach.

J.M.

A Multidimensional Curriculum Design for Speech-Pronunciation Instruction

Past and Present Pronunciation Instruction

Pronunciation teaching in ESL is alive and increasingly well today after a prolonged period of being, quite literally, out of sight and out of mind in many programs. A renewal of interest has flourished as specialists in pronunciation have explored some new and fruitful directions in pronunciation teaching theory, pedagogy, and research over the past few years.[1] Interest in these new developments in principles and practices has spread far beyond the inner circle of known champions of pronunciation.

Some Conventional Wisdom About Pronunciation

A fundamental characteristic of current perspectives in "new-look" pronunciation programs is an expanded conceptualization of the subject as an integral part of oral communication—a part of the entire speech communication act, not something set aside in a drill-bound laboratory. For too long ESL conventional wisdom has maintained that

- Pronunciation isn't important.
- Students will pick it up on their own.
- You can't teach it anyway.
- I don't know how to teach it, even if I wanted to (i.e., I do not have the training).

Below I consider the wisdom of each of these notions.

Pronunciation isn't important?   Brown (1991) noted that one can claim, as did Abercrombie (1956) and Strevens (1974), that *all* language teaching involves pronunciation teaching. Specifically, Abercrombie observed that

> whatever the age and stage of the students, teachers will time and again find themselves tackling questions of pronunciation; whether they do it well or badly,

whether they are satisfied with their handling of it or not—there is no escaping it. . . . (p. 87)

And Strevens (1991) commented,

In the realm of pronunciation, the interrelations between learning and teaching are intricately entwined. Every word, every syllable, every sound uttered by the teacher may contribute to the learning of pronunciation, not only when the teacher is deliberately and overtly concentrating on teaching pronunciation, but equally when he believes that he is putting the weight of the teaching onto questions of grammar or vocabulary, or when he is just easing the class along by an exchange of greetings, or telling a little story. (p. 96)

Of course pronunciation is important—critically important—and especially if it is *your* pronunciation, as an ESL speaker, and *people can't understand you!* Moreover, unless nonnative speakers (NNSs) are comfortably intelligible, they often avoid speaking interactions as much as possible, thus depriving themselves of the learning and practice effects of interaction. It is well documented that speakers with poor intelligibility have long-range difficulties in developing into confident and effective oral communicators; some never do. In addition, the development of competence in oral communication figures importantly in the global dynamic of L2 proficiency, not to mention the complementary role it plays in enriching the breadth and depth of literacy skill development.

Taking a broader perspective on the importance of pronunciation, Beebe (1978), in a paper titled "Teaching Pronunciation: Why We Should Be," observed that in this era of emphasis on meaningful communication, ESL professionals should note that ". . . pronunciation—like grammar, syntax, and discourse organization—*communicates;* . . . the very act of pronouncing, not just the words we transmit, is an essential part of what we communicate about ourselves as people . . . (p. 3; italics added).

Students will pick up pronunciation on their own? Yes, there is some truth in this statement. However, even a quick assessment of a class of adult ESL students will reveal that not all students—in fact, perhaps not very many—have picked up pronunciation satisfactorily on their own and developed into intelligible, confident oral communicators. But more important, denied instruction, learners are deprived not only of systematic endeavors to improve their oral language skills but of systematic approaches to helping them develop personal oral language learning strategies. (See Table 4 for details on learning strategies.)

Pronunciation can't be taught? When one clearly defines what one means by *teaching*, then just as clearly pronunciation *can* be taught and *is* being taught—if, that is, by teaching one means serving as a facilitator (i.e., a speech coach, not a drillmaster) in each learner's personal quest to develop new and/or altered speech-pronunciation patterns—toward becoming a first-rate speaker of English as an L2. (See Table 4 below.)

In searching for a productive way to contextualize learners' development and stabilization of new speech patterns, the University of Michigan's English for Academic Purposes (EAP) program (described below) designed a dual-focus instructional model that combines discrete points of speech production (i.e., specific elements of pronunciation) and general characteristics of speech performance (i.e., global elements of communicability). This instructional perspective simultaneously focuses on a micro level (discrete elements of pronunciation) and a macro level (global elements of communicability and oral discourse in specific settings).[2] Although it is true that the two levels are, in fact, inseparable (the macro encompasses the micro; the micro serves the macro), in practical terms it has proved efficient and effective to frame instruction within this dual focus. (See Table 2 below.)

You don't know how to teach pronunciation? Now that is a serious problem. Some teacher-training programs have developed a new-style communicative pronunciation component in their curriculum, but sadly many programs continue to give very short shrift to the teaching of the pronunciation aspect of oral communication, perhaps because many teacher trainers themselves do not have strong backgrounds in this area. In any case, rather than ignoring such a gap in training, the practical solution for ESL professionals is to participate in conference and in-service training sessions and to do some self-instruction using some of the excellent teacher reference books and new student texts now available in order to develop a comfortable level of expertise in this area. (See Morley, 1991, pp. 487–488, 509–512, for suggestions.)

Why Has Interest in Pronunciation Programs Spread?

Two factors have figured prominently in a renewed interest in pronunciation teaching. One is a growing recognition of *learner problems and unmet learner needs*—in particular, rapidly increasing numbers of adult and near-adult ESL learners whose urgent needs for intelligible, first-rate speaking skills are not being met. The second factor is the emergence of *new instructional designs* in pronunciation teaching. The hallmark of the model followed in many new pronunciation programs is twofold: (a) a considerably broadened conceptualization of what constitutes the domain of pronunciation and (b) practices anchored firmly in current language-learning and -teaching theory. These programs do not slavishly follow rigid methodologies; they develop their own. The basic plan includes the following elements:

A Multidimensional Curriculum Design 69

1. careful diagnostic assessment of learner needs (both micro and macro)
2. careful specification of both short- and long-range goals, in consultation with the learner
3. preparation of both group and individualized instructional syllabi
4. implementation through a variety of instructional activities and appropriate speech-pronunciation communicative tasks.

Learner Problems and Unmet Learner Needs

Clearly, many different groups of adult and near-adult NNSs have poor to unintelligible speech patterns that may place them at serious risk educationally, occupationally, professionally, and socially. As noted elsewhere (Morley, 1991, 1988; Wong, 1985), significant numbers of such potentially disadvantaged speakers of English are found in a variety of settings. For the TESL field to shrug off the needs of these learners is an abrogation of professional responsibility. (See the section on conventional wisdom above.)

What are the speech-pronunciation problems that may disadvantage these speakers of English as an L2? What are the elements of verbal communication that, in the words of Bolinger (1986), "do not communicate *what* the speaker wants, *when* the speaker wants" (p. 2)? NNSs may experience several kinds of problems, including the following:

- *Complete breakdown in communication.* Speech is incomprehensible. Verbal patternings are such that they prohibit functional oral communication. Often these NNSs exhibit extensive breakdown at the micro level that precludes assessment at the macro level. (See the descriptions of ratings 1 and 2 in Table 3.)
- *Ineffectual speech performance.* Speech patterns result in basically ineffectual performance, whatever the intended interlocutor role, whatever the discourse function (e.g., interactional or transactional, in Brown and Yule's terms, 1983). Speakers are judged to lack credibility and do not inspire confidence in either their knowledge of content or their persona. Breakdowns are usually a combination of micro- and macrolevel features.
- *Negative judgments about personal qualities.* Speech patterns result in negative judgments about personality traits and "foreignerism" stereotyping. Beebe (1978) reported that native speakers described pronunciation errors as sounding "'comical,' 'cute,' 'incompetent,' 'not serious,' 'effeminate,' or 'childish'" (p. 3).
- *Anticipatory-apprehensive listener reactions.* When engaging in a conversation with a NNS who had speech-pronunciation problems, native speakers reported having very uncomfortable apprehensive feelings as

the interaction proceeded. Even though they seemed to understand what the NNS was saying at the moment, they felt a continual undercurrent of anxiety, apprehensive that they would not understand as the interaction moved along. Often, they reported, they kept to superficial social topics (i.e., interactional discourse, in Brown and Yule's [1983] terms), shifted topics frequently, spoke more loudly and more slowly, and moved to terminate the interaction as soon as possible.

- *Pejorative stereotyping.* Listener-perceived aberrant speech patterns result in an even more serious negative-judgments problem. That is, NNSs often are assigned undesirable characteristics based on pronunciation. The research of Lambert in Montreal (1967) and Labov in New York (1972) demonstrated that listeners judge speakers they have never seen nor met before as to their personality, intelligence, ethnic group, race, social status—even their height—simply from listening to the way they pronounce a few words (Morley, 1993).

New Directions in Instructional Design

The second factor that has stimulated interest in pronunciation teaching is new developments in instructional design. These innovations are leading toward the reestablishment of pronunciation as a valued and credible component of ESL instruction. Making the case for a new look at pronunciation in the ESL curriculum is full of challenges but has its rewards.

Challenges. A first challenge is one of *designing new-wave pronunciation programs* that reconceptualize principles and expand the pedagogical horizons of pronunciation instruction to meet the demands of today's state-of-the art L2 instruction (see the next section). Reconceptualization encompasses certain instructional features (discussed in the section on designing a multidimensional speech-pronunciation program).

A second challenge is one of *providing proof of the program's value*, that is, demonstrating that new programming leads to learner success. The challenge here lies in convincing colleagues in the profession that a revised pronunciation approach works. This is no easy task; it is an uphill battle against the force of more than 20 years of ESL history that largely holds pronunciation teaching to be a waste of time and to be doomed to failure on at least two counts. First, it is faulted for its traditional beliefs about the nature of language learning and for the style of its language teaching, specifically that rooted in the British system of situational language teaching or the U.S. audiolingual methodology of the 1940s and 1950s. It is also flawed by virtue of the fact that old ways are seen to be in direct conflict with current theory and pedagogy (e.g., today's focus on communicative language teaching, its explicit attention to language functions as well as language forms, learner self-involvement, and learning strategies training).

Rewards. The rewards are found in meeting the challenges—by designing an instructional framework that features practices anchored solidly in an up-to-date belief system and by learner outcomes that show a high degree of learner success for the time invested.

Learner outcomes in an updated pronunciation program must take the form of two acquisition patterns:

1. *Learner process.* Learners must learn how to become positively self-involved, how to become an active forceful partner in their own learning, and how to develop personal skills and strategies for monitoring and altering their own speech patterns.

2. *Learner product.* Learners must demonstrate more intelligible and nondistracting patterns of speech (microlevel features) and/or increasingly satisfactory levels of communicability (macrolevel features); they must have command of speech-monitoring abilities and speech modification strategies that they can use beyond the classroom. Table 3 below illustrates one method of assessing the intelligibility and communicability of the learner's speech.

Expanding the Horizons of Pronunciation Teaching: Shifts in Perceptions and Practices

Changing Focus

The goals of traditional pronunciation teaching procedures appeared to focus primarily—often exclusively—on the area of competence that Canale and Swain (1980) designated *linguistic competence*, in this case phonetic-phonological competence. In contrast, current trends are moving toward practices that also take into account three additional areas of communicative competence: *discourse competence, sociolinguistic competence,* and *strategic competence* (see Table 4).

Yule (1990) has commented that if the class is called *pronunciation* class, one can expect to find a focus on "getting-the-sounds-correct" exercises, but if a class is called *spoken English* class, then one can expect to find a focus on "getting-the-message-across" activities. Today successful new-wave pronunciation programs appear to be making a serious business of a principled combination of these two goals. That is, spoken English class is also partly pronunciation class; pronunciation class is also partly spoken English class. This is the case in the University of Michigan program (discussed below), in which the curriculum includes a series of oral communication courses, some focusing more on speaking skills and some more on pronunciation skills but always in combination. As noted above, overall the program pays active attention to the development of four areas of communicative competence.

Expanding the Horizons

In a recent state-of-the-art discussion, Morley (1991, pp. 492–495) reviewed some of the major shifts in instructional focus in the pronunciation component of ESL.

- *A communicative focus:* a focus that views the proper place of pronunciation in the L2 curriculum as an integral part of communication, not as a separate component set aside from the mainstream
- *An expanded focus on suprasegmentals:* a redirection of priorities within the sound system to a focus on the critical importance of suprasegmentals and how they are used to communicate meaning in spoken discourse, as well as the importance of vowel and consonant sounds (segments), their combinations, and their reduced, elided, and/or assimilated forms
- *An expanded domain for pronunciation:* a focus on an expanded concept of what constitutes the domain of pronunciation that incorporates attention to (a) segmentals; (b) suprasegmentals; (c) voice quality features, articulatory settings, and other paralinguistic areas; and (d) elements of body language used in oral communication (i.e., extralinguistic features)
- *Changing perspectives on the roles of learner and teacher:* a focus on revised expectations for both learner involvement and teacher involvement with an emphasis on the development of the learner strategies of speech awareness, self-awareness, and self-monitoring under the guidance of a speech-pronunciation teacher-facilitator
- *Practice activities aligned along specific-purposes contextualizations:* a focus on practice activities and speaking-task experiences matched to the communicative needs of learners in personalized, real-life contexts
- *Renewed focus on the reciprocal listening-speaking connection:* a renewed focus on the link between listening comprehension and speech-pronunciation (i.e., "How you *hear* English is closely connected with how you *speak* English" [Gilbert, 1984, p. 3])
- *Special attention to sound-spelling relationships:* a focus on a range of important sound-spelling relationships and specific guidance for students on using English orthography as a key tool in predicting pronunciation patterns (Dickerson, 1989; this volume)
- *Individualization and the uniqueness of each learner:* a focus on individualization in the speech-pronunciation class, specifically on the unique-

ness of each ESL learner; each learner has created a personal pattern of spoken English that is unlike that of anyone else, the product of a variety of influences. Instruction needs to guide each learner in his or her unique development of effective communication while attending to the elimination of distracting speech elements.

A Multidimensional Speech-Pronunciation Program

Since 1987 the English Language Institute at the University of Michigan has focused exclusively on the development of a comprehensive curriculum in EAP. Currently over 30 courses are offered, with one credit for a short course (with reduced contact hours per week) and two credits for a regular-length course. The 30 courses are distributed as follows: 10 written communication courses, 11 oral communication courses, 6 international teaching assistant courses, 4 special summer courses, and 2 integrated courses for conditionally admitted students.

The philosophy in the oral communication curriculum at the University of Michigan has been to take the pronunciation class out of isolation, conceptually as well as practically, where it often has been set aside out of the mainstream, and to reconstitute it in both form and function as an integral part of oral communication.

In this section I outline six instructional features of the course work in three of the oral communication courses that focus on communicative pronunciation work (see Table 1).

Instructional Feature 1: A Dual-Focus Program Philosophy

A philosophy of pronunciation teaching as an integral part of communication leads to a dual-focus framework. One focus is on a micro level, with attention to the discrete elements of pronunciation that contribute to improved intelligibility and a goal of developing linguistic competence (specifically, phonetic-phonological competence). The other focus is on a macro level, with attention to general elements of communicability in particular settings and a goal of developing discourse competence, sociolinguistic competence, and strategic competence (see Canale & Swain, 1980; Canale, 1983).

Micro level. As shown in Table 2, at the micro level instruction focuses on (a) contextualized modification of vowel and consonant sounds (including reductions, combinations, and assimilations); (b) the features subsumed under the rubric of stress, rhythm, and intonation; and (c) features of rate,

Table 1
Summary Descriptions of Three Intermediate-Advanced EAP Pronunciation Courses

ELI 336: Pronunciation I
The first in a two-course sequence; 1 credit
- An introductory pronunciation course; intensive work with English vowels and consonants and their combinations and basic features of English stress, rhythm, and intonation; two classes and one tutorial session weekly
- Contextualized practice with two goals: (a) to enable students to modify pronunciation patterns and achieve more intelligible speech and improved oral communication, and (b) to guide students in developing self-monitoring in language learning and self-help strategies to use after formal course work ends (especially metacognitive strategies of planning, monitoring, and checking outcomes)
- A focus primarily on microlevel, discrete-point pronunciation work; some attention to macrolevel, global communicative work

ELI 337: Pronunciation II
The second in a two-course sequence; may be exempted by 336 teacher; 1 credit
- A focus on continuing the work begun in 336; in whole-class sessions, attention to elements of stress, rhythm, and intonation; in small-group and tutorial sessions, attention to extended contextual practice with sounds and sound combinations
- Special attention to individual needs through videotaping and critiquing (especially in tutorials) and through self-study programming designed for each student
- Special attention to metacognitive strategies of self- and peer monitoring and critiquing

ELI 338: Voice and Articulation: Effective Speaking Skills
1 credit
- An intermediate-advanced pronunciation-speaking class; a focus on stabilizing altered pronunciation and integrating modified speech patterns into extemporaneous speaking
- A dual-focus syllabus with more attention to macrolevel elements of oral communicability and less attention to microlevel, discrete-point pronunciation work
- Work on both preplanned and rehearsed speaking practice and extemporaneous speaking practice, often with interactive audience participation in question-and-answer follow-up sessions
- Special attention to individual needs through videotaping and critiquing (especially in tutorials) and through self-study programming designed for each student

Table 2
Dual Focus: Speech Production and Speech Performance

Micro Level Speech Production: Discrete Points (A focus on specific elements of pronunciation)[a]	Macro Level Speech Performance: Global Patterns (A focus on general features of communicability)[b]
• Clarity and precision in articulation of consonant and vowel sounds • Consonant combinations both within and across word boundaries; elisions; assimilations • Neutral vowel use; reductions; contractions • Syllable structure; phrase groups and pause points; linking words across word boundaries • Overall rate of speech; variations in pacing; rhythm, stress, and unstress • Overall volume; sustaining energy level across an utterance; intonation patterns and pitch change points; vocal qualities	• Overall precision and clarity in contextualized speech, both sounds and suprasegmentals • General vocal effectiveness in oral discourse; communicative use of vocal features • Overall fluency in ongoing planning and structuring of speech as it proceeds • Overall speech intelligibility level (see Table 3) • General communicative command and control of grammar • General communicative command of vocabulary words and phrasal units • Overall effective use of appropriate and expressive nonverbal features of oral communication

Note. Revised from Morley (1992, Chart 1, p. xiii). [a]Discrete-point pronunciation features: vowels, consonants, and base features of stress, rhythm, and intonation. [b]General elements and global patterns of communicability in spoken English.

volume, and vocal qualities. Communicative activities stabilize students' emerging abilities to adjust vowel and consonant pronunciation and to manipulate prosodic and vocal features at will with ease and accuracy in order to express their intended meaning and increase their intelligibility.

Macro level. At the macro or global level the program focuses on the synthesis of many components of communicative oral discourse, including (a) overall precision and clarity of speech, (b) discourse-level vocal effectiveness, (c) enhanced ability to sustain speech (i.e., for fluent ongoing structuring and planning of speech as it proceeds), (d) the development of aspects of overall intelligibility, (e) increased communicative command of grammar, (f) an expanded vocabulary of words and phrasal units, and (g) appropriate and expressive nonverbal behaviors. The Speech Intelligibility/Communicability Index in Table 3 is a six-level intelligibility scheme for describing speech and evaluating the way it affects communication.

Table 3
Speech Intelligibility/Communicability Index for Describing Speech and Evaluating Its Impact on Communication

Level	Description	Impact on Communication
1	Speech is basically unintelligible; only an occasional word or phrase can be recognized.	Accent precludes functional oral communication.
2	Speech is largely unintelligible; great listener effort is required; constant repetitions and verifications are required.	Accent causes severe interference with oral communication.
	Communicative Threshold A	
3	Speech is reasonably intelligible, but significant listener effort is required because of the speaker's pronunciation or grammatical errors, which impede communication and distract the listener; there is an ongoing need for repetition and verification.	Accent causes frequent interference with communication through the combined effect of the individual features of mispronunciation and the global impact of the variant speech pattern.
4	Speech is largely intelligible; although sound and prosodic variances from the NS norm are obvious, listeners can understand if they concentrate on the message.	Accent causes interference primarily via distraction; the listener's attention is often diverted away from the content to focus instead on the novelty of the speech pattern.

continued

Instructional Feature 2: Communicative Learner Goals

Traditional expectations, unrealistic goals, and false standards. Many traditional pronunciation texts exhort students to strive for perfect pronunciation, near-native pronunciation, or mastery of pronunciation—and if these expectations are not stated explicitly, they are almost certain to be implied. Although these goals may sound attractive to many students and teachers, the road toward these high levels of perfection is a rocky one—for both parties.

At best perfectionist performance goals are unrealistic because they are virtually unattainable for the vast majority of ESL learners. At worst they

Table 3 Continued

Level	Description	Impact on Communication
	Communicative Threshold B	
5	Speech is fully intelligible; occasional sound and prosodic variances from the NS norm are present but not seriously distracting to the listener.	Accent causes little interference; speech is fully functional for effective communication.
6	Speech is near-native; only minimal features of divergence from NS speech can be detected; near-native sound and prosodic patterning.	Accent is virtually nonexistent.

Notes on Speech Evaluation
1. Elicit a speech sample of several minutes. The sample should be sustained impromptu speech, not just answers to simple questions or "rehearsed" biographical comments. The sample should be spontaneous speech, perhaps on a topic such as (a) what the student wants to be doing in 5 years, (b) what makes the student's life interesting, or (c) what makes a happy family.
2. Try to listen to the speech sample as if you were an untrained language listener. Err on the conservative side with consideration of the "lay" listeners whom the student will meet.
3. In a few descriptive phrases summarize the student's strengths and weaknesses in three areas: (a) use of vowel and consonant sound segments, including combinations, reductions, contractions, elisions, assimilations, and so forth; (b) use of features of stress, rhythm, and intonation, and vocal quality features, rate, volume, and so forth; and (c) features of general communicability (use Table 2 as a reference). Comment on how each of these factors affects communicative intelligibility and assign a Speech Intelligibility/Communicability Level (SI-CL), using [+] and [-] notations as necessary. Monitor student progress through periodic SI-CL reevaluations. Give students practice in the analysis of intelligibility and communicability of speech so that they are equipped to carry out both self-assessment and peer critiquing.
Note. Revised from Morley (1992), p. xv.

have been instrumental in imposing and perpetuating false standards. And aspiring to false standards can be devastating; it can defeat students who feel they cannot measure up and frustrate teachers who feel they have failed in their job.

In fact, there is a widely held consensus that few persons, especially those who learn to speak an L2 in their teens or later, can ever achieve nativelike pronunciation in that L2. How fortunate that perfect or nativelike pronunciation is *not* a necessary condition for fully functional communication in an L2. This is particularly significant in today's world, where English has become an increasingly useful international lingua franca between two NNSs or between a NNS and a native speaker (NS). All around the world this fact is being well documented as hundreds of thousands of NNSs are engaged in

Table 4
Learner Goals, Communicative Competence, and Self-Help Language-Learning Strategies

A. Learner Speech-Pronunciation Goals

1. *Functional intelligibility.* The intent is to help learners develop spoken English that is (at least) reasonably easy to understand and not distracting to listeners. (See Table 2.)
2. *Functional communicability.* The intent is to help the learner develop spoken English that serves his or her individual communicative needs effectively for a feeling of communicative competence.
3. *Increased self-confidence.* The intent is to help learners become more comfortable and confident in using spoken English and to develop a positive self-image as a first-rate nonnative speaker of English and a growing feeling of empowerment in oral communication.
4. *Speech-monitoring abilities and speech modification strategies for use beyond the classroom.* The intent is to help learners develop speech awareness, personal speech-monitoring skills, and speech adjustment strategies that will enable them to continue to develop intelligibility, communicability, and confidence outside class as well as inside.

B. Communicative Competence

The four goals listed in part A are intended to move learners toward developing communicative competence in the following four areas (see Canale & Swain, 1980):

1. *Linguistic competence.* The focus is on sentence-level language with attention to form (i.e., the grammar, the phonology, the lexicon of the L2, etc.).
2. *Discourse competence.* The focus is on discourse above the level of the sentence (i.e., language organization, rhetorical markers, ways of showing relationships in extended oral and written texts, etc.).
3. *Sociolinguistic competence.* The focus is on manipulating language as appropriate to a specific context (i.e., situation, participants, roles, shared knowledge, etc.).
4. *Strategic competence.* The focus is on compensating for weaknesses in any of the other three competence areas (i.e., manipulating language as necessary to cope with breakdowns in communication, to repair miscommunication, etc.).

C. Language-Learning Strategies

The four goals listed in part A also encompass a focus on helping learners develop a variety of language-learning strategies, including the following (see Wenden, 1985; Oxford, 1990):

- *Metacognitive strategies* pay attention to planning, monitoring, and checking outcomes; self-directing language learning.

continued

Table 4 Continued

C. Language-Learning Strategies *continued*
- *Cognitive strategies* focus on intellectual tools; measures that help learners figure out how oral components of the L2 work in various interactions; ways to develop facility in using what has been learned.
- *Communication strategies* focus on compensating for limitations; tools and techniques learners can use when they have "gaps" and miscommunication problems.
- *Global practice strategies* focus on ways learners can seek out speaking practice opportunities and make them happen in the real world.
- *Affective strategies* focus on ways learners can give themselves emotional support, encourage themselves, and lower their anxiety level.
- *Social strategies* pay attention to practicing interactive communication routines; ways to get and give interpersonal support; ways to collaborate, cooperate, and empathize with others (see Oxford, 1985, 1990; Wenden, 1985, 1991).

---

satisfactory communicative interactions in a variety of educational, business, political, and social contexts despite the fact that only an infinitesimal number have perfect pronunciation.

The key to achieving satisfactory communicative speech-pronunciation patterns lies in four areas:

1. functional intelligibility
2. functional communicability
3. self-confidence in using spoken English
4. ability to monitor and modify speaking patterns.

Table 4 presents descriptions of learner goals, communicative competence, and language-learning strategies.

Instructional Feature 3: An Integrated Approach Paradigm of Instructional Objectives and Learner Involvement

Within communicative approaches to pronunciation teaching, teachers must focus on critical dimensions of learning and formulate learning objectives that involve the learner as a whole person. The integrated approach paradigm in Table 5 outlines three dimensions of learning: cognitive or intellectual involvement, affective or psychological involvement, and physical or performative involvement.

Information objectives serve the cognitive dimension of learning and relate to the intellectual component of learning. Attention to intellectual frame-

Table 5
An Integrated Approach Paradigm of
Instructional Objectives and Learner Involvement

A. Cognitive-Intellectual Component of Learning: Information Objectives
1. Language information (*cognitive* strategies)
   a. Speech awareness and long-range goals
   b. Study awareness and short-range goals
2. Procedural information (*metacognitive* strategies)

B. Psychological-Affective Component of Learning: Affective Objectives
1. Learner self-involvement (*cognitive, metacognitive*, and *affective* strategies)
   a. Recognition of self-responsibility
   b. Development of self-monitoring skills
   c. Development of speech modification skills
   d. Recognition of self-accomplishment
2. Comfortable, supportive classroom atmosphere (*affective* and *social* strategies)
   a. Fosters supportive teacher-student interactions
   b. Fosters supportive student-student interactions

C. Physical-Performative Component of Learning: Practice Objectives
1. Speech-pronunciation practice with a focus on integration of components
   a. Linguistic components (phonetic/phonological patterning)
   b. Paralinguistic components (vocal communication strategies)
   c. Extralinguistic components (body and gestural communication)
2. Pronunciation-oriented listening practice (*metacognitive* strategies)
3. Spelling-oriented pronunciation practice (*cognitive* strategies)

Note. Revised from Morley (1992, Chart 3, p. xiv).

works seems to help adult and near-adult learners enormously. Information objectives are intended to help learners develop speech awareness and study awareness in order to engage their intellectual involvement in the learning process. The following two types of information are very useful:

1. *Language information*, which takes the form of short, carefully selected speech-pronunciation descriptions and explanations (to aid learners in developing speech-awareness and speech-modification skills) as well as pronunciation-spelling information and analysis tasks (to help learners unlock some of the mysteries of sound-spelling interpretation and to help them reduce spelling-pronunciation infelicities)

2. *Procedural information*, which includes explicit directions and goal-related participatory guidelines (to help students develop study aware-

ness and to help them understand what they will do, how they will do it, and why it is important).

Students can develop a useful degree of speech awareness and study awareness in a surprisingly short time. Even very young students profit from a little information presented in brief descriptions and simple figures and diagrams. Simplicity, selectivity, and moderation are the keys to effective use of both language information and procedural information.

Affective objectives serve the powerful psychological component of learning. The first critical part of the affective dimension, *learner self-involvement*, is essential as speech-pronunciation study is most profitable (and most pleasant) when students are actively involved in their own learning, not passively detached repeaters of drills. Research has shown that self-involvement is a primary characteristic of good language learners. However, learner self-involvement cannot be left to chance; it must be actively shaped, early and continually, throughout course work. Teachers and materials can help students become involved in the following four areas:

1. *Recognition of self-responsibility.* Teachers can guide learners toward taking responsibility for their own work not just by exhorting them, but by providing ways and means: (a) clear directions and explicit participatory guidelines so that students know the what, the how, and the why; (b) carefully defined tasks, outcomes, and responsibilities for class and small-group activities; and (c) substantive and sharply focused cues for self-monitoring and modifying speech and pronunciation.

2. *Development of self-monitoring skills.* Self-monitoring can begin as gentle consciousness raising with the goal of helping students develop speech awareness, self-observation skills, and a positive attitude toward them (a) by giving concrete suggestions for monitoring (i.e., observing) their own speech on one or two production or performance points at a time, (b) by helping them develop a simple self-rehearsal technique—"talking to yourself and listening to yourself"—as the way to self-monitor, and (c) by helping them shift gradually from the dependent mode of *teacher*-monitoring (in imitative practice and guided self-practice) to the independent mode of *self*-monitoring (in independent rehearsed practice and extemporaneous speaking practice).

3. *Development of speech modification skills.* It is, of course, the learner, not the teacher, who modifies (i.e., corrects) features of speech and pronunciation. It is important to help learners develop a positive understanding of roles: The student's role is to modify (i.e., alter or correct) a microlevel or macrolevel feature of speech or pronunciation; the teacher's role is to give cues to help students identify what, where, and

how to modify and to give support, encouragement, and constructive feedback. Early on, it is useful for teachers to shift from repeated modeling to cueing for student modification.

4. *Recognition of self-accomplishment.* Improvement is a gradual process with much variability and a measure of backsliding from time to time. It is neither an overnight phenomenon nor an all-encompassing development. Learners may find it difficult to notice changes in their own speech patterns, making it imperative that they become aware of small successes in modifying a specific feature of pronunciation or speech on a particular speech task. Many teachers use audio and/or video recordings to guide students in recognizing speech changes in themselves and in their classmates. Assessment of achievement should be based on degrees of change, not absolutes. The emphasis should be on self-comparisons over time, not on student-to-student comparisons.

The second critical part of the affective component is that of fostering a *comfortable supportive classroom atmosphere.* In speech-pronunciation work, perhaps more than in any other part of language study, a comfortable classroom atmosphere is essential for maximum achievement. Classroom interactions need to be enjoyable and supportive and focus on strengths as well as weaknesses. The learning climate needs to be one in which even the most retiring (and the most unintelligible) students can lose their self-consciousness and embarrassment about sounding "funny" as they work to modify speech-pronunciation features. The following two areas are critical:

1. *Supportive teacher-student interactions.* (See Instructional Feature 6 below.)
2. *Supportive student-student interactions.* The Intelligibility/Communicability Index (Table 3) can be very useful in helping students assess their own strengths and weaknesses and those of others. Pair and small-group analysis of specified speech production and/or speech performance features on audio- or videotape can be very effective, but critiquing must be constructive, not destructive, with an emphasis on positive features as well as features that need modification.

Practice objectives serve the physical component of learning. This objective is the performative dimension of speech-pronunciation study and includes the following three kinds of practice:

1. *Speech-pronunciation practice.* For maximum effect, speech-pronunciation instruction must go far beyond imitation; it calls for a mix of practice activities. Three kinds of speech practice can be included from the very beginning: (a) imitative practice, as needed (dependent

practice); (b) rehearsed practice (guided self-practice and independent self-practice); and (c) extemporaneous speaking practice (guided and independent self-practice).
2. *Pronunciation-oriented listening practice.* Specialized speech-oriented listening tasks can help learners develop their auditory perception, their discriminative listening skills for dimensions of speech-pronunciation communicability, and their overall aural comprehension of English. Attention needs to be given to prosodic features and vocal features, including the fast-speech phenomena found in authentic speech patterns as well as vowel and consonant sounds and their combinations.
3. *Pronunciation sound-spelling practice.* ESL students must learn to relate spoken English and written English quickly and accurately if they are to become truly literate in English. A variety of sound-spelling work can prepare them to do this. An awareness of spelling patterns as cues to stress and rhythm patterning can be tremendously useful to learners (see Dickerson, 1989, this volume).

Instructional Feature 4: Curriculum Guidelines for Instructional Planning

Using the dual-focus model to reach the learner goals and meet the learning objectives, the University of Michigan's speech-pronunciation curriculum encompasses the assessment and instruction components outlined in Table 6.

Imitative practice should be used only as necessary. In fact, it may be best utilized as an embedded component within the context of rehearsed or extemporaneous practice, especially with advanced or intermediate students. The purpose of modeling-and-imitation activities is to focus on controlled production of selected speech-pronunciation features (see Table 7). Such activities can include in-class work, self-access audio- or videotaped materials for individual use or for assigned pair and small-group study sessions outside class, or speech-analysis computer programs that transform speech input into visual displays on the computer screen. Imitative practice should not be used beyond the point where a learner can produce the given feature(s) easily at will; speaking practice should then shift immediately to rehearsed and extemporaneous activities.

Rehearsed speaking practice serves as a practice mode in its own right as well as an interim step between imitative and extemporaneous practice. The purpose is to stabilize modified speech-pronunciation patterns (either micro, discrete-point features or macro, global features) so that the learner becomes skillful in manipulating them easily at will. Rehearsed practice uses relatively fixed texts, such as oral reading scripts of a wide variety selected

Table 6
Curriculum Guidelines for Instructional Planning: Assessment and Instruction

A. Assessment

1. *General Comments*
   Use the Speech Intelligibility/Communicability Index and other evaluations of speech-pronunciation and levels of intelligibility and communicability.

B. Practice

1. *General Comments*
   Use cycles of three modes of speech-pronunciation practice: imitative, rehearsed, and extemporaneous. These three speech practice modes range across three levels of learner dependence-independence:
   - *Dependent practice*
     Mode: imitative speech practice with model given
   - *Guided practice*
     Mode: rehearsed speech practice using oral script-reading and/or rehearsed presentations
   - *Independent practice*
     Mode: extemporaneous speech practice with the content self-selected (i.e., self-generated) by the learners so that it meets their personal, educational, and/or career needs or their own English for specific purposes needs

2. *Three Modes of Pronunciation Practice*
   - *Imitative speech practice*

Purpose:	to establish controlled production of selected speech-pronunciation features
Speech Activities:	contextualized work with microlevel features of pronunciation (both sound segments and suprasegmentals) and macrolevel features of communicability (see Table 2)
Strategy Goals:	attention to the development of *metacognitive* and *cognitive* strategies

continued

or composed by teachers or students (e.g., simulated radio or television broadcast scripts of all kinds; excerpts from famous speeches, plays, narrative poems, novels, role-play skits, and playlets; and preplanned, relatively short oral presentations of a wide variety, with topics selected by students). Activities include

- in-class, audio- or videotaped dress rehearsal and final performance (with feedback critique sessions held either immediately or later)

Table 6 Continued

- *Rehearsed speech practice*

  Purpose: to stabilize altered or new speech-pronunciation features

  Speech Activities: use of relatively "fixed" texts (both oral reading scripts and preplanned talks), out-of-class self-study rehearsals, and both in-class rehearsals and one-on-one work sessions with the speech coach

  Strategy Goals: attention to the development of *social, metacognitive*, and *communication* strategies

- *Extemporaneous speech practice*

  Purpose: to integrate modified speech patterns into naturally occurring creative speech

  Speech Activities: both partially planned and unplanned talks, panel discussions, and interactive audience dialogue in a question-and-answer format or reaction-and-comment format

  Competence Goals: attention to developing *linguistic, discourse, sociolinguistic,* and *strategic* competence

C. Learning Strategies and Teaching Strategies
See Tables 7 and 8.

- out-of-class, audio- or videotaped self-study rehearsals or paired and small-group rehearsal study sessions
- one-on-one individual speech workout study sessions with the speaking teacher (i.e., speech coach).

Rehearsed practice can move into the next mode (extemporaneous speech practice) with the addition of audience-participation question-and-answer and discussion interactions.

Table 8 gives some useful monitoring checkpoints and learning strategies for either rehearsed or extemporaneous speech practice.

Extemporaneous speech practice helps students integrate their modified speech patterns into naturally occurring creative speech in both partially planned and unplanned talks (monologues). Examples of activities are

- small-group panel discussion presentations, both formal and informal (preplanned outside class, or planned relatively spontaneously during class time in small-group work sessions and presented immediately)
- audience-interaction follow-up "dialogue" sessions in a question-and-answer format

Table 7
Student Learning Strategies for Imitative Speech Practice

1. **Strong, Vigorous Practice; Slightly Exaggerated Practice**
   Listen and watch carefully. Use vigorous practice with strong muscular movements. Use slightly exaggerated practice of articulatory movements and contacts. Don't hurry. Take time to articulate clearly.

2. **Self-Monitored Practice**
   Listen closely and monitor yourself on both the sounds and the rate, rhythm, and vocal qualities. Duplicate stress points, pitch rises and falls, and rhythmic patterns—exactly.

3. **Slow-Motion Practice; Half-Speed Practice**
   Try slow-motion—or half-speed—practice for a strong sense of kinesthetic touch-and-movement feedback and for the feeling of articulation.

4. **Loop Practice ("Broken Record" Practice)**
   Use an endless-loop practice of 20 or more strong and vigorous repetitions of a phrase or word with focus on kinesthetic feedback.

5. **Whisper Practice (Silent Practice)**
   Use whispered or silent practice to focus, once again, on the feeling of articulation.

6. **Mirror Practice; Video Practice**
   Use mirrors to view the articulation of a specific sound. If available, close-up video filming and subsequent viewing are useful.

Note. Revised from Morley (1992, Chart 4, p. xvi).

- in-class, audio- or videotaped presentations
- out-of-class self-study rehearsals individually, in pairs, or in small-group preparation sessions
- audio- or videotaped one-on-one individual workout speech sessions with the speech coach, followed by feedback sessions.

As noted in Table 6, these practice modes move from *dependent* practice (with a model given), to *guided* practice (with self-initiated rehearsed speech), to *independent* practice (with both partially planned and extemporaneous speech practice) with the content self-generated and developed by the learners to meet their needs.

Table 8
Student Monitoring Checkpoints and Learning Strategies for Rehearsed and Extemporaneous Speech Practice

ABOVE ALL
- Don't whisper!
- Use strong, vigorous speech!

1. **Articulation**
   Use careful, precise articulation. Take time to articulate clearly. Don't mumble or swallow your speech.

2. **Rate**
   Use controlled speed and pause by phrase groups. Take time to slow your rate of speech and vary your tempo. Don't speed up just to get finished.

3. **Stress and Rhythm**
   Use clear emphasis—with a few appropriate stress points and intonation rises—but don't overuse emphasis. Establish the rhythmic stress-unstress pattern of English including reductions and contractions; link words into phrase groups across word boundaries.

4. **Volume, Intonation, and Voice Quality**
   Use a moderate loudness level. Don't whisper. Don't shout.
   Keep your energy level up (i.e., sustain your energy level) to the end of an utterance.
   Use a moderate intonation range with appropriate change points of pitch rises and pitch falls.
   Use lively, expressive voice qualities.

5. **Self-Monitoring and Self-Correction**
   Monitor your speech. Take every opportunity to modify a pronunciation point, as necessary, in an easy and matter-of-fact manner.

Note. Revised from Morley (1992, Chart 5, p. xvi).

Instructional Feature 5: The Learner's Role

Adult learners seem to learn best when they are involved consciously in the speech modification process as they work to become intelligible, communicative, confident speakers of English. Teachers can assist learners in developing the useful attitudes and types of awareness listed below.

1. speech awareness
2. self-awareness of features of speech production and speech performance

3. self-observation skills and a positive attitude toward self-monitoring processes
4. speech-modification skills
5. awareness of the learner's role as one of a speech performer modifying, adjusting, or altering a feature of speech-pronunciation, and the teacher's role as one of assisting students as a speech coach
6. a sense of personal responsibility for one's own learning, not only for immediate educational and personal needs but for future career needs
7. a feeling of pride in one's own accomplishments
8. the construction of a personal repertoire of speech-monitoring and speech-modification skills in order to continue to improve speaking effectiveness in English when the formal instructional program is finished.

As noted, explicit attention to training in learning strategies is an essential part of the University of Michigan's speech-pronunciation curriculum. Such training fosters speech awareness (a cognitive component of learning), self-monitoring (a metacognitive component of learning), and self-modification of speech patterns (a practice-metacognitive-cognitive component).

A primary goal is to involve students consciously in their own learning process as they work to modify their spoken English. Each part of each lesson focuses students' attention on what they are doing, why they are doing it, and how to do it. Lessons encourage personal involvement by providing students with

- ways and means (a) to take responsibility for their own work and (b) to take a personal pride in their many small accomplishments along the way toward improved spoken English
- tools and techniques with which (a) to monitor others and themselves, (b) to modify their spoken English in bits and pieces, and (c) to continue to improve their spoken English when they leave the formal classroom and language laboratory (Morley, 1979, pp. vii, viii).

Instructional Feature 6: The Teacher's Role

Programs that are committed to helping learners modify speech-pronunciation patterns and develop effective speech skills often reflect a philosophy of the learner-teacher partnership. In pronunciation work, perhaps more than in any other facet of L2 instruction, clearly the teacher does not teach but facilitates learning in a very special learner-centered way.

The teacher as speech-pronunciation coach. In programs with the partnership philosophy, the role of the teacher is to assist learners—like a speech-pronunciation coach. The work of a speech-pronunciation coach approximates that of a debate coach, a drama coach, a voice coach, a music coach, or even a sports coach, who characteristically supplies information; gives models from time to time; offers cues, suggestions, and constructive feedback about performance; sets high standards; provides a wide variety of practice opportunities; and supports and encourages the learner.

The speech-pronunciation coach has the critically important role of monitoring and guiding modifications of spoken English in speech production (the micro level) and speech performance (the macro level). Note again that articulatory phonetics is not thrown out but takes a place as one part in the larger communicative picture of getting the message across.

Teacher responsibilities. The teacher-as-coach has a challenging task made up of diverse responsibilities:

1. conduct speech-pronunciation diagnostic analyses, and choose and give priority to those features that will make the most noticeable impact on modifying the speech of each learner
2. help students set both long-term and short-term goals
3. design the scope and sequence of the group program; design personalized programming for each learner in the group
4. develop a variety of instructional formats, modes, and activities (e.g., whole-class instruction, small-group work, one-to-one tutorial sessions, prerecorded audiotaped and/or videotaped self-study materials, computer-assisted programs); provide genuine speech tasks for practice situated in real contexts and carefully chosen simulated contexts
5. structure in-class speaking (and listening) activities with NS and NNS guests
6. plan field trip assignments in pairs or small groups for real-world speaking practice
7. monitor learners' speech production and speech performance at all times and assess changes in pattern as an ongoing part of the program
8. encourage student speech awareness and realistic self-monitoring
9. always support each learner in his or her efforts, be they wildly successful or not so successful.

A Concluding Note

Today's professional commitment to the learner—to empowering learners, enabling them to succeed not just survive, assisting learners in becoming effective, fully participating members of the English-speaking communities in which they communicate—has created a need for first-class speaking skills vis-à-vis functional intelligibility and functional communicability. Pronunciation must therefore be written back into the instructional equation, but with a new look following the premise that *intelligible pronunciation and global communicability are essential components of communicative competence*.

Notes

1. See, for example, the papers by Browne and Huckin (1987); Catford (1987); Celce-Murcia (1987); Crawford (1987); Gilbert (1987); Temperley (1987); Wong (1987); and the other papers in this volume, among others.

2. In the Michigan program, the macro focus is on EAP as used for specific purposes within a variety of university academic contexts.

References

Abercrombie, D. (1956; reprinted, 1991). Teaching pronunciation. In A. Brown (Ed.), *Teaching pronunciation: A book of readings* (pp. 87–95). London & New York: Routledge.

Beebe, L. (1978). Teaching pronunciation: Why we should be. *IDIOM*, 9, 2–3.

Bolinger, D. (1986). *Intonation and its parts*. Palo Alto, CA: Stanford University Press.

Brown, A. (Ed.) (1991). *Teaching pronunciation: A book of readings*. London & New York: Routledge.

Brown, G., & Yule, G. (1983). *Discourse analysis*. New York: Cambridge University Press.

Brown, H. D. (1994). *Teaching by principle: An interactive approach to language pedagogy*. Englewood Cliffs, NJ: Prentice-Hall.

Browne, S., & Huckin, T. (1987). Pronunciation tutorials for nonnative technical professionals: A program description. In Morley (1987), pp. 1–57.

Canale, M. (1983). From communicative competence to communicative language teaching. In J. Richards & R. Schmidt (Eds.), *Language and communication* (pp. 2–27). London: Longman.

Canale, M., & Swain, M. (1980). Theoretical bases of communicative approaches to second language teaching and testing. *Applied Linguistics*, 1, 1–47.

Catford, J. C. (1987). Phonetics and the teaching of pronunciation: A systemic description of English phonology. In Morley (1987), pp. 87–100.

Celce-Murcia, M. (1987). Teaching pronunciation as communication. In Morley (1987), pp. 1–12.

Crawford, W. (1987). The pronunciation monitor: L2 acquisition considerations and pedagogical priorities. In Morley (1987), pp. 105–120.

Dickerson, W. (1989). *Stress in the speech stream: The rhythm of spoken English.* Urbana & Chicago: University of Illinois Press.

Gilbert, J. (1984). *Clear speech: Pronunciation and listening comprehension in American English.* New York: Cambridge University Press.

Gilbert, J. (1987). Pronunciation and listening comprehension. In Morley (1987), pp. 29–39.

Labov, W. (1972). *Sociolinguistic patterns.* Philadelphia: University of Pennsylvania Press.

Lambert, W. (1967). A social psychology of bilingualism. *Journal of Social Issues,23,* 91–109.

Morley, J. (1979). *Improving spoken English.* Ann Arbor: The University of Michigan Press.

Morley, J. (Ed.) (1987). *Current perspectives on pronunciation: Practices anchored in theory.* Washington, DC: TESOL.

Morley, J. (1988). How many language do you speak? Perspectives on pronunciation-speech-communication in EFL/ESL. *Nagoya Gakuin University Roundtable on Linguistics and Literature Journal, 19,* 1–35. Nagoya, Japan: Nagoya Gakuin University Press.

Morley, J. (1991). The pronunciation component in teaching English to speakers of other languages. *TESOL Quarterly, 25,* 481–520.

Morley, J. (1992). *Extempore speaking practice.* Ann Arbor: The University of Michigan Press.

Morley, J. (1993). Learning strategies, tasks, activities in oral communication instruction. In J. Alatis (Ed.), *Strategic interaction and language acquisition: Theory, practice, and research.* Washington, DC: Georgetown University Press.

Oxford, R. (1985). *A new taxonomy of second language learning strategies.* Washington, DC: ERIC Clearinghouse on Languages and Linguistics.

Oxford, R. (1990). *Language learning strategies.* New York: Newbury House.

Strevens, P. (1991). A rationale for teaching pronunciation: The rival virtues of innocence and sophistication. In A. Brown (Ed.), *Teaching English pronunciation: A book of readings* (pp. 96–103). London & New York: Routledge.

Temperley, M. (1987). Linking and deletion in final consonant clusters. In Morley (1987), pp. 59–82.

Wenden, A. (1985, Spring). Learner strategies. *TESOL Newsletter,* pp. 4–5, 7.

Wong, R. (1985). Does pronunciation teaching have a place in the communicative classroom? In D. Tannen & J. Alatis (Eds.), *Language and linguistics: The interdependence of theory, data, and application* (pp. 17–28). Washington, DC: Georgetown University Press.

Wong, R. (1987). Learner variables and pre-pronunciation considerations in teaching pronunciation. In Morley (1987), pp. 17–28.

Yule, G. (1990). Reviews of J. Kenworthy, R. Wong, and J. Morley. *System, 18,* 107–111.

— 6 —

Recent Research in L2 Phonology: Implications for Practice

Martha C. Pennington
City Polytechnic of Hong Kong

Editorial Notes

In the introduction to her paper, Martha Pennington lists six themes that have emerged as important areas of research in L2 phonology. Characterizing these themes as "autonomous but partially overlapping," she presents a clear and informed discussion of current research in each area. She includes sufficient detail to be of value to the nonspecialist as well as the specialist in L2 phonology and provides insightful notes on implications for practice.

In *phonology in context* Pennington observes that in current theory, patterns of oral discourse are conceptualized as a linguistic level of spoken language that lies between the content and the sound segment; that is, a bridge that connects the meaning encoded in the spoken discourse to the phonetic level. From this view it follows that informed instructional planning for phonological instruction in an L2 must focus first on the discoursal context in which the speech is embedded and second on appropriate prosodic patternings at various levels (e.g., phrase, clause, sentence, larger segment of discourse).

Pennington then moves to a discussion of *phonological parameters*, the set of features that comprise an L1 speaker's underlying linguistic model, whose values govern the surface structure (i.e., phonetic level) of speech actualization. These parameters appear to be language specific and are believed to exert a powerful underlying influence on a speaker's production of L2 sound segments. In Pennington's words, these features "may be defined in terms of parameters carried over from the L1 into the L2 and in need of readjustment for phonological fluency and accuracy in an L2." This process, which has come to be called a parameter-resetting model, may be a useful way to introduce learners to L1 and L2 values and to help learners understand L1/L2 differences.

The *transfer and development* discussion presents a synopsis of Major's views on interlanguage phonology (1987) and the related work of other researchers. Central to Major's model is the thesis that there is a series of predictable stages in the acquisition of L2 phonology. In the first stages of the learning process the most prominent feature is the influence of interference from the L1. In subsequent stages this influence appears to diminish, giving way to what Major calls developmental processes, noting that these processes also decrease in still later stages of L2 phonological acquisition. These two processes affect L2 acquisition in ways that are manifested in the differential types of error patterns learners exhibit as they move through stages in their individual acquisition of L2 phonology. Pennington stresses the importance of recognizing these influences so that appropriate teaching materials and activities can be developed to provide different instructional frameworks at different times.

Critical features of the interrelationships between *speech perception* and *speech production* are discussed next, with a review of research on learners' need to adjust and readjust their categories of both perception (sensory futures) and production (motor features). In maturational constraints Pennington examines issues relating to the controversial topic of age and language acquisition. She suggests that teachers may want to design different kinds of practice experiences that accommodate to learners' capabilities at different ages.

In a key section at the end of the paper Pennington discusses several new studies that have investigated psychological and social influences on L2 accent. Traditional textbooks often listed "a nativelike accent" as a primary goal of pronunciation study; legions of disappointed students (and their teachers) have asked "Why? Why does a nativelike accent seem to be achievable by so few L2 speakers?" The research reported here suggests that factors of self-image and language identity may exert a very strong influence on the nativelike quality of accent. Pennington presents a number of implications for practice in the final part of this section.

J.M.

Recent Research in L2 Phonology: Implications for Practice[1]

Paralleling a similar surge in the development of phonological theory within linguistics, L2 phonology is a rapidly growing area of research and practice in L2 learning and teaching. From a review of recent research in L2 phonology, six partially autonomous and partially overlapping themes emerge as important foci of attention:

1. phonology in context
2. phonological parameters
3. transfer and development
4. perception and production
5. maturational constraints
6. psychosocial factors.

Below new research in each of these areas is summarized as a basis for drawing implications for language teaching and pedagogical research. It is concluded that, because one's pronunciation patterns are a form of habitual behavior manifested in several dimensions at once, pronunciation instruction must follow multiple approaches.

Phonology in Context

The prosodic or suprasegmental level of language has increasingly come to be seen as a linguistic level standing at a position intermediate between segmental phonology and connected discourse, linking individual sounds with higher linguistic units. It has been argued that the nonsegmental features of stress, rhythm, pitch, intonation, and general articulatory setting may be the determining factor in the achievement of nativelike segmental phonology while limiting the possibilities for achieving full social and discourse competence (Chun, 1988a, 1988b; Esling, this volume; Pennington, 1989, 1990; Pennington & Richards, 1986). Indeed, it can be argued that "the acquisition of phonological competence and discourse competence go hand-in-hand" (Pennington, 1990, p. 549) as the language learner over time becomes increasingly able to manipulate grammatical patterns, lexicon, and segmental and suprasegmental phonology to achieve different social and aesthetic purposes.

Context—including local and distant (discourse-level) linguistic context as well as social context (who is talking to whom and the circumstances of talk)—thus constrains pronunciation. By implication, phonology must be taught in context: Segments should be contextualized by suprasegments, and suprasegments should be contextualized by discourse of different types. At the same time, comparative research is badly needed on different approaches to teaching phonology in context. A recent study by del Castillo (1990) did not show any advantage for a focus on phonology using a prosodic approach in place of standard listening comprehension materials. However, del Castillo speculated that the materials she used to train the subjects in suprasegmental phonology, which largely followed Gilbert's (1993) popular *Clear Speech* course, may not have provided adequate practice. In the future, different and more extensive approaches to training phonology in context should be developed and tested with different populations of learners.

Phonological Parameters

As a specific type of linguistic contextual constraint, high-level or deep-level features such as the orientation of phrasal and sentential accent have been proposed as underlying a host of other systemic features that ultimately determine the production of individual phonemes in a particular language (Donegan & Stampe, 1983; Selkirk, 1984). These may be defined in terms of parameters carried over from the L1 into the L2 and in need of readjustment for phonological fluency and accuracy in an L2 (Pennington, 1987, 1990). From this perspective, "foreign accent" can be characterized as speaking the L2 with L1 phonological settings.

Within second language acquisition (SLA), the parameter-setting model can be seen as a new incarnation of contrastive analysis that may or may not have any psychological reality in relation to the learner's internal processing strategies (James, 1990, p. 184). As James (1990) has noted, "the interpretation of [the value of parameters] for explaining SLA is crucially dependent on what processing status we give them in foreign language learning" (p. 182). The typical case in L2 acquisition seems to be that learners approach new values for phonological features gradually and piecemeal, rather than as the outcome of a rapid shift or early-stage resetting of underlying or midlevel parameters required for pronouncing the L2 like a native speaker (Pennington, 1990).

Thus, a parameter-resetting model, though useful as a metaphor for L2 acquisition, may not actually apply in the literal sense intended for parameter setting in L1 acquisition theory. Nevertheless, such a model does offer a useful way of representing the "phonological distance" that a learner must travel from the pronunciation values of the L1 to those of the L2. For pedagogical purposes, the parameter-setting framework might then be a useful teaching tool for helping learners to understand differences between the L1 and the L2. It also furnishes a theoretical basis for attempting radical approaches to L2 instruction (e.g., those of Gattegno, 1978, in the Silent Way or of Neufeld, 1978, in his perception training experiments) that aim to set (or reset) basic L2 phonological parameters at the beginning stage of language learning before directing attention to meaning or syntax.

Based on a parameter-setting model, it can be hypothesized that "learners who are able to reset underlying or general parameters early on will achieve better results in L2 acquisition than those who develop each aspect of the interlanguage system individually" (Pennington, 1990, p. 541). Language pedagogy would therefore benefit from investigations of the nature and the chronology of the deep-level parametric shifts required for mastery of English by speakers of languages with a very different phonological basis and the success or failure of learners in achieving these shifts.

Moreover, if it is true that certain general parameters constrain low-level or surface-level phonological features, teaching the pronunciation of segmental phonemes without attention to the relevant high-level or deep-level features should be highly inefficient. Comparative research should be able to test the efficiency of teaching with reference to various general phonological parameters versus teaching with a focus exclusively on segment-level phonology. Such research would be of considerable value in determining appropriate teaching approaches for L2 phonology. This type of research program also offers an indirect way of evaluating the validity of parametric models for L2 phonology.

Transfer and Development

In one of the most influential articles in L2 phonology in recent years, Major (1987) proposed an Ontogeny Model for L2 phonological acquisition. According to this model, *interference processes*, which predominate in the early stages of SLA, gradually decline and make way for *developmental processes*, which increase in the middle stages of acquisition and decrease in later stages. According to Major (1987), under conditions of spontaneous speech, when the learner attends more to content than to form, interference from the L1 appears in the surface forms of L2 utterances. L1 transfer (in the form of interference) may thus be more common in informal production tasks such as spontaneous speech than in formal production tasks such as reading a word list. The developmental constraints of natural phonological processes, such as lenition (weakening) or fortition (strengthening), and other general developmental processes, such as simplification or overgeneralization, also affect the L2 learner's phonological production in different speaking styles. As an example, Major (1987) noted that

> a Portuguese speaker's pronunciation of word-final consonant clusters in English might depend on style. The operation of the two common developmental processes, schwa insertion and consonant cluster simplification (neither of which is a process in native Portuguese), might depend on the style of the speaker. The schwa insertion (e.g., [rostəs] *roasts*) would be expected more frequently in a more formal style than would consonant cluster simplification [ros]). This is because schwa insertion is a fortition process that *insures* that the final consonants are perceived, whereas consonant cluster simplification is a lenition process [i.e., one which aids production]. (p. 108; italics in original)

In a related point, Weinberger (1987) argued that addition of a schwa vowel (schwa epenthesis) to a word ending in a consonant ensures the *recoverability* of the underlying form of an utterance, whereas deletion of a final consonant makes it difficult for the listener to recover the underlying form. Therefore, a speaker will be less likely to delete a final consonant—and so more likely to select a production strategy, such as schwa epenthesis, that preserves the underlying form—in decontextualized conditions such as reading a word list aloud. At the same time, according to Weinberger's (1987) reasoning, the speaker will be more likely to delete final consonants in circumstances such as reading aloud or telling a story when context ensures a good chance of recoverability of the underlying form of the word, even if it is uttered in an abridged form. Other authors (e.g., Edge, 1991; Pennington & Ku, 1993) have pointed out that the type of developmental strategy, such as epenthesis or deletion, may be constrained by the phonological system and sociolinguistic choices provided by the L1.

In attempting to explain the consistent patterns and the variation in L2 phonological acquisition, researchers have further explored the intricacies of transfer and developmental processes in terms of *dominant* and *recessive* relationships to phonological proficiency (Pennington, 1990), degree of *transferability* (Hammarberg, 1990), and variation in the *trajectories* of different phonemes in L2 phonological development (Wieden, 1990). Each of these explorations has found that some phonological features have stronger effects than others on the phonology of the L2, thus emphasizing the nonuniform nature of transfer and developmental phenomena.

Phonological transfer and developmental processes thus appear to operate in complex ways in L2 phonology, causing learners to make a variety of errors at different stages and under different task constraints in producing the L2. Rather than trying to inhibit them from making these errors, it may in fact be more valuable to organize the language classroom so that learners are given many and varied opportunities to:

1. produce language—and therefore to make errors—in a range of speaking tasks, and then
2. receive feedback to assist them in adjusting those productions.

Research on L2 grammar supports the value of first "leading learners down the garden path" by inducing them to overgeneralize grammatical patterns or to base L2 grammatical solutions on L1 transfer and then correcting their errors. Other research has shown that feedback on some types of errors aids acquisition in communicative language-learning situations (Lightbown & Spada, 1990). L2 researchers could extend the domain of this research to phonology by explicitly comparing various approaches for preproduction (inhibitory) and postproduction (corrective) strategies in L2 phonological pedagogy and by systematically investigating which types of phonological errors are most responsive to corrective feedback.

Perception and Production

In learning an L2, "Well-formed perceptual targets may be a necessary condition, but are not a sufficient condition, for productive success: the requisite motor programs must also be available" (Leather & James, 1991, p. 318). In the acquisition of an L2 sound system, the successful learner must adjust both the perceptual targets and the motor programs for speech production to the values required for nativelike performance. During the course of acquisition, as the learner attempts to make the appropriate adjustments, perception relates to production in different ways and constrains it to different degrees.

In computer-based lessons enhanced with visual representations of Chinese tone, Leather (1990) demonstrated a strong interrelationship between phonological perception and production, in that "training in one modality tended to be sufficient to enable a learner to perform in the other" (p. 95). At the same time, much recent research has demonstrated that the relationship between phonological production and perception is neither a simple, bidirectional, causal relationship nor a one-to-one correspondence of proficiencies. In a study conducted by Boatman (1989, 1990) on the acquisition of French vowels by adult L2 learners, correlations between phonological perception and production, and between phonological competence and grammatical competence, varied considerably depending on the type of task (e.g., discrimination versus labeling). Leather and James (1991) conclude:

The collective findings of a variety of investigations . . . do not constitute clear evidence of any constant and simple correspondence between perception and production—which should therefore not be viewed merely as two sides of the same coin. An alternative view is that the speech learning system has sufficient versatility to interrelate perceptual and productive knowledge in the most fruitful way permitted by particular—and often changing—circumstances. (p. 320)

Leather and James (1991, p. 316) suggest that in producing a new sound system, the learner moves progressively from moment-by-moment, "on-line," feedback-regulated (*closed-loop*) control of speech to cognitively preprogrammed (*open-loop*) control achieved by a motor program, or plan. Ongoing monitoring and moment-by-moment control of phonology demand considerable attention on the part of the learner and thus slow down speech production, whereas preprogramming means that articulatory gestures execute themselves quickly and automatically, thus increasing fluency. In the view of these authors:

A "best-fit" model of the process of L2 speech sound learning would perhaps represent the learner's primary goal as the construction of phonetic prototypes to which the processes of both perception and production may be geared. These prototypes, or parametric representations, would capture the central acoustic tendencies of "good" tokens. They would serve both perceptual decisions . . . and production activity . . . by means of schemata (i.e., structured plans) that define the serial and hierarchical orderings of the requisite cognitive and motor events . . . , providing . . . for successive decisions in perception and the activation of articulatory plans with feedback-based adjustments in production. The hypothetical association of independent perceptual and productive schemata with an L2 phonetic prototype may be sufficient to account for apparent divergences between a learner's perception and production of a given sound. . . . (Leather & James, 1991, p. 320)

In SLA, phonetic prototypes may at first be based on L1 prototypes, which are gradually altered based on input from and practice with the L2.

Recent studies in L2 phonology (e.g., Baptista, 1990; Bohn & Flege, 1990; Major, 1987; Pennington, 1990) illustrate how learners adjust and readjust their categories of perception and production in the course of learning a new language. In a typical pattern of development, the adjustment process proceeds from well-defined and tightly constrained initial targets to more broadly defined and loosely constrained targets in the middle stages of acquisition, which are then gradually refocused into well-defined new targets in the later stages of acquisition. As the number and types of errors increase at middle stages of acquisition (Hammarberg, 1990; Wieden, 1990), the effects of the readjustment process may appear regressive. In his computer-based research on Chinese tone, Leather (1990) found evidence that acquisition of tone proceeds by fits and starts, noting that:

There is no clear evidence here that learners' gains in productive ability over the whole course of a training stage were monotonic and gradual for each of the tones. . . . As seemed to be the case for perceptual learning . . ., the apparent "setbacks" . . . reflect patterns of learning in which a modification to a provisional prototype for one of the four tones engenders changes in parameters or features elsewhere in the learner's evolving tone system. (pp. 88–89)

Like human evolution in general, evolution of a sound system seems to proceed in terms of discontinuous change events punctuating periods of systemic equilibrium. Clearly, learners need a considerable amount of speaking practice to establish and automatize articulatory routines in a new language. They also need a great deal of exposure to authentic models of the phonology of an L2 to develop nativelike perceptual targets for L2 speech. Leather (1990) has emphasized the need for learners to practice and to receive feedback on their developing perceptual and productive abilities in pronunciation:

Without the opportunity for testing a developing prototype in perception and/or production, the learner might cease at an early stage to exploit his [/her] potential for progressively modifying or fine-tuning his [/her] model. Given usable feedback, on the other hand s/he [sic] may make successive improvements to the accuracy of each evolving prototype until progress comes asymptotically to an end. (p. 96)

Because individual phonemes do not develop in isolation, it seems important to expose learners to phonemes in the context of the whole phonological system and not only as individual, isolated items. It also seems valuable to expose learners to the pronunciation of phonemes in a wide variety of contexts and not only to the most common or central exemplar of each sound. In this connection, Leather (1990) has stressed the importance in learning of adequate exposure to different speakers' voices:

The present perceptual learning data underline the need for the learner to have access to sets of exemplars that collectively span an appropriate range of interspeaker variation. Too much or too little variability at too early a stage may prevent the learner from discovering with sufficient accuracy the prototypical forms that exemplars expound. (p. 96)

Maturational Constraints

In a number of recently published books and articles (Flege, 1987, 1988, 1990; Harley, 1986; Johnson & Newport, 1989; Long, 1990; Major, 1990; Scovel, 1988; Singleton, 1989; Snow, 1988), the ongoing controversy about age and language acquisition rages on. Authors such as Scovel (1988), Long (1990), and Major (1990) have stressed the impossibility of acquiring an accent-free L2 after childhood because of biologically based neurological changes. According to Flege (1990), however, such an explanation leads to a paradox:

> Why should most sensorimotor skills increase through adolescence but those underlying speech learning decrease? . . . I think it [most] likely that the basic processes and mechanisms that guide successful speech learning during L1 acquisition remain intact well into adulthood, but that foreign accent persists in the speech of many adults who learn an L2 because of factors that are independent of basic speech learning abilities. (p. 255)

In the view of Leather and James (1991):

> That some ontogenetic neurological change limits the ability of adults to learn a new sound system is not proven . . ., nor should the lateralization hypothesis preclude alternative or complementary explanations of age-related differences in learners' success with L2 speech—as might, for instance, be formulated in terms of wider sociocultural and general maturational factors. (p. 307)

Echoing the view of Flege (1987, 1988, 1990), Leather and James (1991) propose the following:

> A less limiting explanation for the widely reported disadvantage of adults in learning new sound systems might . . . be that ontogenetic modification between childhood and adulthood in the perception of non-native phonetic contrasts involves not so much a sensorineural loss as a change in auditory processing strategies. . . . In normal linguistic listening, . . . the available evidence seems to indicate that the crucial respect in which the adult differs from the young child is in having established a greater bias toward phonetic rather than purely sensory perception in linguistically construed tasks and by being correspondingly less likely to make use of simple sensory (pre-phonetic) analyses in inferences about the sound patterns of an L2. (p. 309)

In Flege's (1990) view, a central factor in the development of "foreign accent" is that "the propensity for equivalence classification may increase precipitously about the age of 5–6 years" (p. 257). The older learner's tendency to classify L2 sounds as equivalent to L1 phonemes is the basis for phonological interference. Language teachers should steer clear of teaching approaches and materials that encourage equivalence classification through orthographic or simplified phonemic representations of L2 sounds, for presentations of L2 sounds in terms of orthography or simple phonemic symbols invite equivalence classification of, and thus interference with, L1 sounds. In contrast, a presentation using "exotic" symbols for L2 sounds and stressing phonetic detail will naturally focus the learner's attention on how different, rather than how similar, the sounds of the L1 and L2 are.

Although older learners' tendency toward equivalence classification may work against them in acquiring a nativelike accent in an L2, the mature perceptual capacity to make analogies and to transfer learning from one experience to another is one aspect of the superior learning capabilities of older learners that is evidenced in virtually all dimensions other than exact replication of linguistic utterances (Singleton, 1989). Thus, rather than ignoring older students' learning preferences or tendencies and attempting to make them learn language in the "natural," childlike way, language teachers can capitalize on the skills that adolescents and adults have, such as the ability to compare and contrast and to recognize patterns in input. Moreover, it may be possible to develop the mature learner's ability to self-analyze and self-regulate to the point where they may help to compensate for any tendency to categorize sounds according to previous linguistic experience.

Psychosocial Factors

Psychosocial constraints may operate in L2 phonological acquisition to pressure the L2 learner to pronounce the L2 with a nativelike accent. As Bohn and Flege (1990) observe:

> Perhaps perception of a new vowel contrast is more resistant to L2 experience than production because speech production is more subject to social control than speech perception. Non-native listeners can function adequately if they rely on vowel spectrum and duration to differentiate the English /ɛ/-/æ/ contrast because native English speakers produce both spectral and duration differences between /ɛ/ and /æ/. On the other hand, non-native talkers may feel greater pressure to conform to the production norms of the L2 in order to avoid being stigmatized for misidentifiable or foreign-accented speech. (p. 52)

The more nonnative speakers are responsive to such psychological and social pressure from native speakers, the more they might be expected to modify their targets for production (but not necessarily perception) in the direction of native speaker norms.

Guiora and Schonberger (1990) argued that pronunciation occupies a "unique position . . . in the total web of language behavior," as it defines a unique language identity. In the view of these authors, only one authentic language identity is possible, and this identity is determined less by which language is the chronological L1 or home language than by social conditions such as an overriding social pressure to assimilate within a given speech community. Thus, when they analyzed the speech of 29 high school students living in Israel who:

1. spoke English in their families at home and
2. learned both Hebrew and English in childhood, even those whose English was chronologically prior to their Hebrew,

they found that 25 of them had Hebrew as the dominant language and spoke English, but not Hebrew, with a "slight accent." Summarizing their results, Guiora and Schonberger (1990) state, "Most natural bilinguals . . . were found (a) to produce native pronunciation only in the dominant language, (b) not to speak the dominant language with a foreign accent and (c) to speak the non-dominant language with a slight accent" (p. 30).

The identity signaled by a certain accent sometimes serves as a psychosocial constraint pressuring the nonnative not to speak in a nativelike way in order to avoid any identification with native speakers—including symbolic identification with their sociocultural values. In many cases, the phonology of nonnative speakers may be based on a linguistic model other than Standard English that does not challenge their basic identity in the L1 community. Hence, as Edge (1991) concludes in relation to the English of native Cantonese speakers from Hong Kong, "For many phonetic features, nativized varieties and other non-standard Englishes offer different targets than those of what has been called Standard English . . ." (p. 391). If an L1-influenced phonology has become the institutionalized standard for production of the L2, learners will presumably find it more difficult to acquire nativelike L2 phonology than if both languages have entirely separate identities—as seems to be the case in childhood acquisition of two languages (Cruz-Ferreira, 1990).

Differences in phonology that signal differences in individual and group identity include differences not only in global accent but also in the pronunciation of individual sounds. A pronunciation of a certain sound that signals membership in a certain group is termed a *phonological marker* of identity in that group (Labov, 1972). For example, the way a person pronounces the first vowel of the word *chocolate* is a reliable indicator of whether or not the person grew up in New York City or northern New Jersey as against anywhere else in the United States. This pronunciation can therefore be said to be a marker of membership in the community of speakers who live in New York City or northern New Jersey. As another example, a pronunciation of the word *pattern* as identical to many people's pronunciation of the name *Patton* is a marker of the regional accent of upper New England—Vermont, New Hampshire, and Maine.

In research on stereotyped markers of the phonology of American English and Mexican Spanish, Zuengler (1988) found that very different stereotypes and cues to accent exist in the two groups. To native speakers of Mexican Spanish, the American English /r/ is the most salient marker of an American accent, whereas to American English speakers, the pronunciation of vowels is the most stereotyped marker of a Mexican-Spanish accent. In work on native speakers' attitudes toward the accents of immigrants in Sweden, Cunningham-Andersson (1990) found that the immigrants' pronunciation of some phonemes produced stronger negative reactions in Swedish listeners than the pronunciation of other phonemes did.

Considering that a person's language identity, and hence phonology, is tied up with attitude toward self and one's relationship to the community of speakers of the L1 as well as the L2, work on L2 phonology needs to be tied in with work on the individual's value set, attitudes, and sociocultural schema. Drawing again on older learners' special abilities, teachers can assist mature students to develop an expanded meta-awareness and control of their own affective responses and of the communicative resources available—for example, in the area of voice quality or variable pronunciations of specific phonemes—for interacting with native speakers outside their own community. Part of this training may involve work with L2 learners to produce a variety of laryngeal and supralaryngeal articulatory settings and to recognize the social connotations of their associated voice qualities (Esling, 1987, this volume).

Considering the research on stereotyped markers, teachers should train early and most intensively those features of the nonnative's phonology that cause the most negative reactions in the relevant native-speaker population, perhaps putting off or even disregarding those features that do not elicit strong negative responses in native speakers. As a basis for deciding which features to teach, research is needed to identify those phonological features to which native listeners attend most and react most strongly. Research is also needed on the effectiveness in terms of overall listener response of training selected phonological features rather than more general communicative abilities. For example, comparison of training focused on general communicative effectiveness or intelligibility, such as the usual training given in international teaching assistant (ITA) courses (e.g., Byrd, Constantinides, & Pennington, 1989), with training focused on the most stereotyped phonemes and prosodic features, would be of value for future ITA and other ESL courses.

Conclusion

Based on the foregoing review, the adult speaker's pronunciation patterns can be described as a form of habitual behavior that exists on several levels at once and that is therefore highly resistant to change (Pennington, 1993). When it comes to habits—and pronunciation patterns are no exception—a very short distance exists between "I can't change," "I don't want to change," and "I don't think it's good to change." In the first statement—"I can't change"—generally intended as "It's not possible at my age," the learner expresses a perception of his or her inability to change. This statement is thus a physiologically based rationale for the persistence of the habit. The second statement—"I don't want to change"—is generally intended as "It's too much trouble to change." This rationale is often coupled with one that maintains "I don't *need* to change" or "There is no good reason to change," the implication being that "I communicate well enough as it is." This second statement is an expression of the learner's attitude, a psychologically based rationale for not breaking a habit. The third statement—"I don't think it's good to change"—generally means, "My values make me resist sounding like a native speaker." This statement is clearly one of the learner's values, a socioculturally based rationale for not changing.

Just as in the case of other kinds of habitual behavior, in the case of the phonological habit, the presence of any one of these rationales—whether physiological, psychological, or sociocultural, and whether it represents a real or imagined reason, a conscious or unconscious attitude—presents a major barrier to alteration of long-standing behavioral patterns. When such barriers exist, as they generally do in adult language learning, structured learning experiences may help the learner to become more receptive to and more able to make changes in phonological features and to recontextualize pronunciation at all levels. Instruction can help give learners the perceptual and the productive experience they need to reconceptualize the performance targets while offering motivation to change and social experiences to develop a new value set, that is, a new conceptualization of the psychological and sociocultural target. In this way, approaches to instruction in L2 phonology will be geared not only to training perceptual and productive performance at the level of the physiological habit but also to providing a basis for change in the psychological and social dimensions of pronunciation.

Note

1. A longer version of this paper appeared as *Recent Research in L2 Phonology: Implications for Practice*, May 1992 (Research Report No. 15), Hong Kong: City Polytechnic of Hong Kong, Department of English.

References

Baptista, B. O. (1990). The acquisition of English vowels by Brazilian learners. In H. Burmeister & P. L. Rounds (Eds.), *Variability in Second Language Acquisition, Proceedings of the Tenth Meeting of the Second Language Research Forum* (pp. 187–204). Eugene: University of Oregon.

Boatman, D. (1989). *An investigation of adult second language perception and production: Evidence for and against a predictive account.* Unpublished doctoral dissertation, University of Pennsylvania, Philadelphia.

Boatman, D. (1990). The perception and production of a second-language contrast by adult learners of French. In Leather & James (1990), pp. 57–71.

Bohn, O.-S., & Flege, J. E. (1990). Perception and production of a new vowel category by adult second language learners. In Leather & James (1990), pp. 37–56.

del Castillo, L. (1990). *Pronunciation through prosody.* Unpublished master's thesis, Department of English as a Second Language, University of Hawaii, Manoa.

Byrd, P., Constantinides, J., & Pennington, M. (1989). *The foreign teaching assistant's manual.* New York: Heinle & Heinle.

Chun, D. (1988a). The neglected role of intonation in communicative competence and proficiency. *The Modern Language Journal, 72,* 295–303.

Chun, D. (1988b). Teaching intonation as part of communicative competence: Suggestions for the classroom. *Unterrichtspraxis, 21,* 81–88.

Cruz-Ferreira, M. (1990). Karin and Sofia in bilingual-land. In Leather & James (1990), pp. 248–254.

Cunningham-Andersson, U. (1990). Native speaker reactions to nonnative speech. In Leather & James (1990), pp. 1–13.

Donegan, P. J., & Stampe, D. (1983). Rhythm and the holistic organization of language structure. *Chicago Linguistic Society, 19,* 337–353.

Edge, B. A. (1991). The production of word-final voiced obstruents in English by L1 speakers of Japanese and Cantonese. *Studies in Second Language Acquisition, 13,* 377–393.

Esling, J. H. (1987). Methodology for voice setting awareness in language classes. *Revue de Phonétique Appliquée, 85,* 449, 473.

Flege, J. (1987). A critical period for learning to pronounce foreign languages? *Applied Linguistics, 8,* 162–177.

Flege, J. (1988). The production and perception of foreign language speech sounds. In H. Winitz (Ed.), *Human communication and its disorders* (pp. 22–41). Norwood, NJ: Ablex.

Flege, J. (1990). English vowel production by Dutch talkers: More evidence for the "similar" vs. "new" distinction. In Leather & James (1990), pp. 255–293.

Gattegno, C. (1978). *Teaching foreign languages in schools the silent way.* New York: Educational Solutions.

Gilbert, J. (1993). *Clear speech: Pronunciation and listening comprehension in North American English* (2nd ed.). Cambridge: Cambridge University Press.

Guiora, A., & Schonberger, R. (1990). Native pronunciation of bilinguals. In Leather & James (1990), pp. 26–36.

Hammarberg, B. (1990). Conditions on transfer in phonology. In Leather & James (1990), pp. 198–215.

Harley, B. (1986). *Age in second language acquisition.* San Diego: College Hill Press.

James, A. (1990). A parameter-setting model for second language phonological acquisition? In Leather & James (1990), pp. 180–188.

Johnson, J., & Newport, E. (1989). Critical period effects in second language learning:

The influence of maturational state on the acquisition of English as a second language. *Cognitive Psychology, 21,* 69–99.

Labov, W. (1972). *Sociolinguistic patterns.* Philadelphia: University of Pennsylvania Press.

Leather, J. H. (1990). Perceptual and productive learning of Chinese lexical tone by Dutch and English speakers. In Leather & James (1990), pp. 72–97.

Leather, J., & James, A. (Eds.) (1990). *NEW SOUNDS 90: Proceedings of the 1990 Amsterdam Symposium on the Acquisition of Second-Language Speech.* University of Amsterdam.

Leather, J., & James, A. (1991). The acquisition of second language speech. *Studies in Second Language Acquisition, 13,* 305–341.

Lightbown, P., & Spada, N. (1990). Focus-on-form and corrective feedback in language teaching: Effects on second language learning. *Studies in Second Language Acquisition, 12,* 429–446.

Long, M. H. (1990). Maturational constraints on language development. *Studies in Second Language Acquisition, 12,* 251–285.

Major, R. (1987). A model of interlanguage phonology. In G. Ioup & S. Weinberger (Eds.), *Interlanguage phonology: The acquisition of a second language sound system* (pp. 101–124). New York: Newbury House/Harper & Row.

Major, R. (1990). L2 acquisition, L2 loss, and the critical period hypothesis. In Leather & James (1990), pp. 14–25.

Neufeld, G. (1978). On the acquisition of prosodic and articulatory features in adult language learning. *The Canadian Modern Language Review, 34,* 163–174.

Pennington, M. C. (1987, July). *Universals, prosody, and SLA.* Paper presented at the conference on Second Language Acquisition: Contributions and Challenges to Linguistic Theory, Stanford University, Palo Alto, CA.

Pennington, M. C. (1989). Teaching pronunciation from the top down. *RELC Journal, 20,* 20–38.

Pennington, M. C. (1990). The context of L2 phonology. In H. Burmeister & P. L. Rounds (Eds.), *Variability in Second Language Acquisition, Proceedings of the Tenth Meeting of the Second Language Research Forum* (pp. 541–564). Eugene. University of Oregon.

Pennington, M. C. (1993, August). *Breaking the L1 phonological habit.* Paper presented at the Congress of the International Association for Applied Linguistics, Vrije University, Amsterdam.

Pennington, M. C., & Ku, P.-y. (1993). Realizations of English final stops by Chinese speakers in Taiwan. *RELC Journal, 24,* 71–90.

Pennington, M. C., & Richards, J. C. (1986). Pronunciation revisited. *TESOL Quarterly, 20,* 207–225.

Scovel, T. (1988). *A time to speak: A psycholinguistic inquiry into the critical period for human speech.* Rowley, MA: Newbury House.

Selkirk, E. (1984). *Phonology and syntax.* Cambridge, MA: MIT Press.

Singleton, D. (1989). *Language acquisition: The age factor*. Clevedon, U.K.: Multilingual Matters.

Snow, C. (1988). Relevance of the notion of a critical period to language acquisition. In M. Bornstein (Ed.), *Sensitive periods in development: Interdisciplinary perspectives* (pp. 183–210). Hillsdale, NJ: Lawrence Erlbaum.

Weinberger, S. (1987). The influence of linguistic context on syllable simplification. In G. Ioup & S. Weinberger (Eds.), *Interlanguage phonology: The acquisition of a second language sound system* (pp. 401–417). New York: Newbury House/Harper & Row.

Wieden, W. (1990). Some remarks on developing phonological representations. In Leather & James (1990), pp. 189–197.

Zuengler, J. (1988). Identity markers and L2 pronunciation. *Studies in Second Language Acquisition, 10*, 33–49.

— 7 —

The Effects of Pronunciation Teaching

George Yule
Louisiana State University

Doris Macdonald
Northern Illinois University

Editorial Notes

George Yule and Doris Macdonald focus squarely on a problem of long standing in language teaching in general and of special relevance to the teaching of L2 pronunciation: What are the observable effects of the teaching? What are the measurable changes in the learner's language behavior?

The authors report on a controlled experiment conducted to study changes in learners' pronunciation patterns as a result of specific instructional procedures. Their purpose was to clarify the effects of pronunciation teaching that teachers observe, to describe and classify the changes resulting from that teaching, and to argue that teachers should take more seriously the effects of trying to modify a learner's L2 pronunciation patterns.

Yule and Macdonald made three audiorecordings of ESL learners giving controlled-topic presentations that included targeted vocabulary items. At time one (T1) a before-instruction tape-recording was made, followed immediately by an instructional session, which in turn was followed by a T2 recording. The third recording (at T3) was made 2 days later but with no intervening instruction. Native speakers of American English then judged the pronunciation of key vocabulary words by each subject at the three times.

The pronunciation instruction sessions between T1 and T2 were designed to reflect ESL classroom practices. Group 1 was given a teacher-directed drill activity (the TEACH condition) in which the key words were modeled for repetition, with corrective feedback as needed. Group 2 was given a traditional language laboratory activity (the LAB condition) in which the key words were presented on a tape that the students listened to individually and practiced on their own. Group 3 (the WHAT condition) made their oral presentation to a teacher who asked for clarification of the students' pronunciations of the key words in their presentations. Students in Group 4 (the SIRE condition) were given time to revise their presentation materials silently, with no instruction.

None of the results appeared to favor one teaching technique over another to a definitive degree. The ranking from most to least effective under the four conditions (LAB, WHAT, TEACH, SIRE) should be treated with caution, as differences were not statistically significant. Yule and Macdonald observed the following patterns of behavior across T1, T2, and T3:

- immediate improvement and continued effect
- improvement and maintained effect
- immediate improvement and subsequent reversal
- no improvement
- immediate deterioration
- immediate deterioration and reversal

One important pattern that all teachers need to be aware of is that of the learner whose performance deteriorates immediately but improves later. The authors note that some worsening in pronunciation may mean that the learning process is taking place and that its benefits will show up later.

Clearly, an important interaction exists between the method of instruction and the individual student, and no one method of instruction benefits all individuals equally. According to the authors, the wide range of individual reactions to the type of pronunciation instruction suggests that the individual learner, not the teaching method involved, may be the more powerful variable in studies such as this. Furthermore, the results suggest caution in judging whether instructional procedures are effective, as indications of immediate improvement can disappear after a few days whereas signs of immediate deterioration can be noticeably reversed in the same time span.

J.M.

The Effects of Pronunciation Teaching

Although language teaching is necessarily conducted with the assumption that the techniques and procedures employed will have beneficial effects, the investigation and confirmation of those effects remains problematic. Practicing language teachers easily recognize the phenomenon of instant improvement in a learner's L2 performance as a result of a specific classroom exercise, followed by the disappearance of that improvement not long after when the focus of classroom work has moved on. Some teachers may also be familiar with the opposite effect whereby no improvement is immediately apparent following the exercise, yet later there is a noticeable improvement in the learner's performance on features presented in earlier classroom work.

The latter effect is presumably the more desirable, yet ironically it may be the effect that, on most measures, is rarely recorded. Indeed, on most measures, which consider only the immediate effect, the latter pattern will be recorded as a failure of method whereas the former will be seen as a successful outcome. We suspect that many language teachers, finding no immediate improvement in their learners' performance after some classroom activity, may either abandon the activity or decide that they, as teachers, have failed in some way to implement the activity effectively. This observation may hold for any aspect of language teaching, but it is particularly relevant for the teaching of L2 pronunciation. Many in the language-teaching field seem to feel that pronunciation teaching has little observable effect and that classroom time can be more effectively devoted to fostering other aspects of the L2. Below we present a clearer picture of the observed effects of pronunciation teaching, illustrate the range of patterns of change brought about by that teaching, and argue for a more serious consideration of the complex effects potentially involved when teachers set out to modify a learner's L2 pronunciation.

In the spirit of Morley's recent observation that there is "a need for controlled studies of changes in learner pronunciation patterns as the result of specific instructional procedures" (1991, p. 512), we report on a study that tried to capture different individual reactions to four different instructional practices used in pronunciation teaching. The focus on the individual learner is motivated not only by arguments in the literature (cf. Ellis, 1990; Skehan,

1989) that, in general, L2 learning is very much an individual experience, but also by the fact that, in particular, pronunciation is a crucial aspect of each individual's personal experience, identity, and presentation of self. Nowhere is "the uniqueness of each ESL learner" (Morley, 1991, p. 495) more in evidence than in the patterns of L2 pronunciation adopted, and in no other aspect of L2 learning is it more difficult to account for the complex psychological processes at work in how learners want to present, as well as express, themselves. Consequently, the patterns of change that may be observed in an individual's L2 pronunciation, following some instructional procedure, can be perceived and described but never completely accounted for. The accounts offered here will be tied to the materials used but should nevertheless be treated as necessarily speculative.

The Study

A group of 23 graduate students from the People's Republic of China with relatively high proficiency in written English but noticeable pronunciation problems in spoken English voluntarily took part in this study. They were provided, in advance, with written information containing key vocabulary items on aspects of the metric system (e.g., *temperature, metric, Celsius*), which they used as a basis for oral presentations that were then tape recorded. The first tape-recorded presentation (T1) was followed by a session during which the students received some form of pronunciation instruction before the second tape-recorded presentation (T2). After this second taping, the students were given a new set of related materials on the metric system, containing the same key vocabulary items, and instructed to come to the next class session (2 days later) prepared to make the third oral presentation (T3). Thus we had tape recordings of these students' pronunciations of a number of the same key vocabulary items before instruction (at T1), immediately after instruction (T2), and two days after instruction (T3). Each speaker's pronunciations of specific vocabulary items were paired as instances of T1 versus T2 or as T1 versus T3. Native speakers of American English then listened to a large number of these pairings and decided which of each pair was closest to the American English pronunciation of the word in question. These native-speaker judgments were used to determine whether each student's pronunciation was perceived to be better at T2 than at T1 (or not) and at T3 than at T1 (or not).

The pronunciation instruction sessions between T1 and T2 were designed to reflect ESL classroom practices. Six students took part in a teacher-directed drill activity in which the key words were modeled for repetition, with corrective feedback as needed (the TEACH condition). Six were given a traditional language laboratory activity, with the key words presented on a tape that students listened to individually and practiced on their own, with no teacher present (the LAB condition). Six were placed in the WHAT condition, which required them to make their oral presentation to a teacher who would ask for clarification (typically by saying *What?*) of the students' pronunciations of the key words in their presentations. According to those who argue for the benefits of modified interaction (e.g., Pica, 1988), such prompts to clarify what is said in the L2 will focus the learner on the need to produce more accurate forms. In the final condition, five students were simply given time to silently revise their presentation materials. This will be referred to as the SIRE condition and was included as essentially a control condition to measure what happens when there is no active instruction between T1 and T2. More technical details on the students, procedures, and materials involved in this study are presented in Macdonald, Yule, and Powers (1994).

Immediate Improvement

Most language teachers assume that instruction focused on some forms of the L2 will bring about perceived improvement in the learner's L2 performance using those forms. In our study, this type of effect, where T2 is perceived to be better than T1 (T2 > T1), was found in fewer than half the students. Only seven individuals continued or maintained their immediate improvement. The immediate-and-continued effect resulted in a pattern whereby students continued their immediate improvement from T1 to T2 through T3 (T3 = T2 > T1) (shown in Figure 1A). Three students, one each from the TEACH, LAB, and WHAT conditions, were observed to have derived this extremely desirable effect from the pronunciation instruction they received. Almost as desirable is an improvement-and-maintained effect, illustrated in Figure 1B, showing that students maintain the improved level of performance perceived at T2 until T3 (T3 = T2 > T1). Four students, two each from the LAB and the WHAT conditions, demonstrated this effect. These two conditions, LAB and WHAT, seem to result in more immediate and continued or maintained improvement than either of the other conditions for the particular individuals involved.

Unfortunately, in another observed pattern, illustrated in Figures 1C and 1D, immediate improvement is subsequently reversed. As shown in Figure 1C, some students do not seem to retain the immediate benefits of instruction and revert over time to their initial performance levels (T2 > T3 = T1). This was the case for three students, one each from the TEACH, LAB, and SIRE conditions. Even more disturbing is the pattern in Figure 1D, observed for two students, one each from the TEACH and WHAT conditions, in which initial improvement is reversed to such an extent that the students are

Figure 1
Immediate Improvement

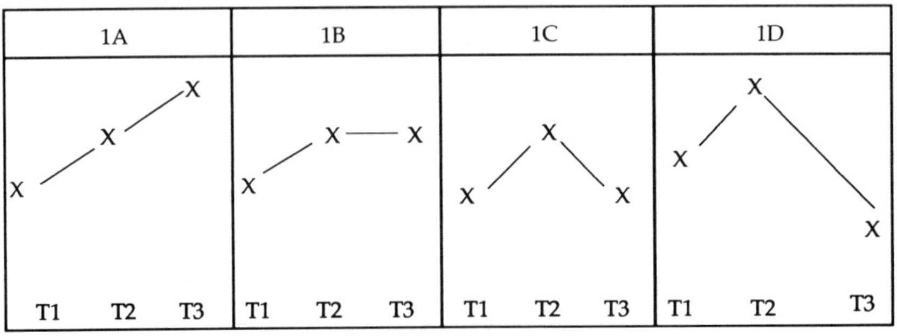

1A	1B	1C	1D
X rising to X rising to X across T1, T2, T3	X rising to X then level X across T1, T2, T3	X rising to X then falling to X across T1, T2, T3	X rising to X then falling sharply to X across T1, T2, T3

perceived to be performing worse than ever by the final point (T2 > T1 > T3). Given that these reversals can occur in the LAB and WHAT conditions despite our earlier observations on their beneficial effects, we infer that there is a crucial interaction between method of instruction and individual student and that no one method of instruction uniformly benefits all individuals. Indeed, a method that brings about immediate and continued improvement in the perceived pronunciation of one individual can equally result in a substantial decline in perceived performance for another individual in the same small group.

Attempting to account for this "reversal" effect in fact leads us to consider the more general but rather infrequently discussed phenomenon of learners becoming *worse* in their L2 performance as a result of instruction. Let us first consider the range of patterns noted when the learners in this study did get worse immediately following the instruction sessions.

Immediate Deterioration

Illustrating the patterns opposite from those in Figures 1A–1D, the effects represented in Figures 2A–2C would be generally undesirable outcomes for any pronunciation teacher. For a student to get worse immediately after some instructional event and then to decline even further beyond the event, as shown in Figure 2A, would lead most teachers to abandon the instructional practice entirely. This effect (T1 > T2 > T3) was observed for one individual in the LAB condition and one in the WHAT condition, and was the majority effect (three individuals) in the SIRE condition. For those three individuals, being left to work on their own with no active pronunciation instruction had an extremely negative effect on their subsequent performance. Intended as a control condition, the silent revision session is clearly not representative of any activity currently promoted for pronunciation teaching. The negative

Figure 2
Immediate Deterioration

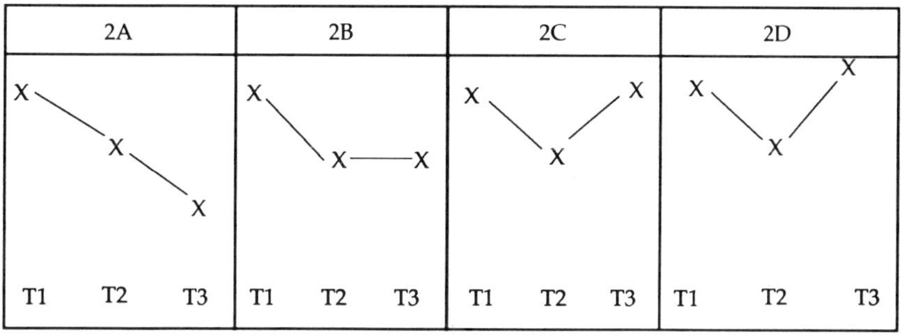

2A	2B	2C	2D
X⟍ X⟍ X	X⟍ ⟍X—X	X⟍ ╱X X	X⟍ ╱X ⟍X╱
T1 T2 T3	T1 T2 T3	T1 T2 T3	T1 T2 T3

effects should nevertheless be treated as a warning that, without a definitive pronunciation activity in connection with their oral presentations, some students are likely to become progressively worse in their level of performance.

Those individuals in the LAB and WHAT conditions whose performance continued to deteriorate are also reminders that any activity involves potentially negative effects. In being left to practice with tape-recorded material (the LAB condition), a student can, of course, be busy practicing forms other than the target forms presented on the tape. When prompted to change an existing pronunciation via a clarification request, as in the WHAT condition, a student may, of course, change that pronunciation to something even further from the target.

The pattern shown in Figure 2B is clearly a possible outcome of pronunciation teaching, but no instances were observed in this study. The reversal pattern shown in Figure 2C (T3 = T1 > T2) was present in one individual's performance in the WHAT condition, and the deterioration-improvement reversal of Figure 2D (T3 > T1 > T2) was found in two individuals, one each in the TEACH and SIRE conditions. This type of pattern is reminiscent of the U-shaped development noted among some language learners (cf. Kellerman, 1985; Yule, Hoffman, & Damico, 1987), with the immediate decline in performance possibly attributable to what McLaughlin (1990) has called *restructuring*. The important concept used to account for the observed decline in performance in such cases is that the instructional event actually disrupts the learner's existing interlanguage, and that it takes time for some restructuring to take place and for the changes to be incorporated. Some caution is clearly required in interpreting any immediate decline in performance as an indication of restructuring taking place, but pronunciation teachers who may be discouraged by that observed decline should keep it in mind. Some deterioration in performance may actually be evidence of the learning process at work, with beneficial effects appearing some time later.

Figure 3
No Immediate Change

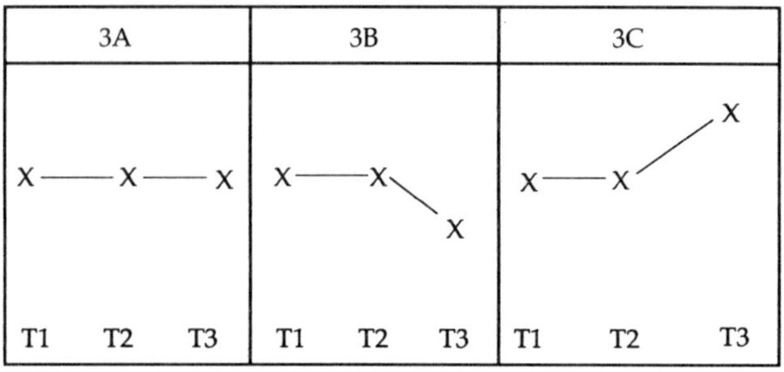

3A	3B	3C
X——X——X	X——X↘ 　　　　X	X——X↗X
T1　T2　T3	T1　T2　T3	T1　T2　T3

No Immediate Change

That same restructuring process may also be taking place among learners whose performance shows no immediate change as a result of pronunciation instruction. Those individuals may simply have been unaffected by the instruction and may have continued to perform at the same level regardless. The pattern of no change whatsoever (T1 = T2 = T3), shown in Figure 3A, was noted for only one learner, in the TEACH condition, and may have something in common with what has been described as "fossilized" L2 pronunciation (Selinker, 1972). In such a case, the type of instruction provided may be irrelevant because the learner's way of using the L2 is impervious to change. However, the absence of immediate change may be connected to the kind of instructional activity presented in the TEACH condition as one other learner in this condition showed no immediate change and then got worse (T1 = T2 > T3), following the pattern shown in Figure 3B.

The only individual who exhibited a beneficial effect after no immediate change (T3 > T2 = T1), following the pattern in Figure 3C, had taken part in the LAB condition. We might consider this pattern as exemplifying some kind of "delayed" effect where the benefits of the instructional event do not become apparent until some time after. This is another case where the longer-term benefit may not be immediately obvious to the teacher and, on most postinstruction measures, would not even be recorded.

Conclusions

The wide range of individual reactions to the type of pronunciation instruction found in this study should serve as a reminder that the individual learner may represent a more powerful variable in such studies than the type of teaching method involved. It may also lend support to Pennington and

Richards' (1986) contention that there is unlikely to be a one-to-one relationship between pronunciation teaching and learning. Moreover, the changes in direction observed in many cases across the three points in time should also make teachers cautious about making premature decisions about the effectiveness (or not) of instructional procedures. Indications of immediate improvement can disappear after a few days, and signs of immediate deterioration can, in the same time span, be noticeably reversed.

A look at the instructional choices presented here leads to some observations on the relative merits of each based on the number of individuals whose T3 pronunciations were perceived to be better than those at T1 per condition. The SIRE condition generally resulted in deterioration, with only one of five learners showing overall improvement. The TEACH condition caused the least change among individuals and resulted in two of the six learners showing overall improvement. The WHAT condition brought about the most substantial continued deterioration in one individual's performance but also led to three of the six learners demonstrating overall improvement. Finally, the LAB condition produced the least deterioration, had two individuals with the most substantial improvement recorded, and resulted in four of the six learners showing overall improvement.

Although more individuals seem to have benefited from the LAB condition in this investigation, these results should be treated with a great deal of caution. The learners in the study were exclusively Chinese, who, as Yule, Wetzel, and Kennedy (1991) have shown, do differ in their reactions to spoken English forms from other L1 learner groups. Also, the articulation of single vocabulary items is only an extremely small part of an individual's overall L2 pronunciation and may be less relevant as a defining feature when other aspects such as sentential rhythm and intonation are taken into account. There is also the matter of time. The changes observed from T1 to T2 to T3 in this study may not have been present if the time intervals had been longer. For example, the restructuring and delayed effects described here may not have been complete for some individuals by the T3 point and, at some later time, could have become more apparent. Alternatively, the immediate and continued or maintained improvement noted for some individuals at T3 could possibly have been reversed at some later point if our investigation had been extended in time.

Bearing these cautionary notes in mind, we nevertheless suggest that this type of study does provide some important insights and some graphic metaphors for thinking about what happens when teachers set out to modify the pronunciation of L2 learners. We hope that, at the very least, we have given L2 teachers some reassurance that initial deterioration in pronunciation after instruction is not necessarily the end of the process and that subsequent improvement is not only one of the possible but also one of the natural effects of pronunciation teaching.

Acknowledgment

A version of this paper will appear in the journal *IRAL* (1995).

References

Ellis, R. (1990). Individual learning styles in classroom second language development. In J. deJong & D. Stevenson (Eds.), *Individualizing the assessment of language abilities* (pp. 83–96). Philadelphia: Multilingual Matters.

Kellerman, E. (1985). If at first you *do* succeed. . . . In S. Gass & C. Madden (Eds.), *Input in second language acquisition* (pp. 345–353). Rowley, MA: Newbury House.

Macdonald, D., Yule, G., & Powers, M. (1994). Attempts to improve English L2 pronunciation: The variable effects of different types of instruction. *Language Learning, 44*, 75–100.

McLaughlin, B. (1990). Restructuring. *Applied Linguistics, 11*, 113–128.

Morley, J. (1991). The pronunciation component in teaching English to speakers of other languages. *TESOL Quarterly, 25*, 481–520.

Pennington, M., & Richards, J. (1986). Pronunciation revisited. *TESOL Quarterly, 20*, 207–226.

Pica, T. (1988). Interlanguage adjustments as an outcome of NS-NNS interaction. *Language Learning, 38*, 45–73.

Selinker, L. (1972). Interlanguage. *IRAL, 10*, 209–231.

Skehan, P. (1989). *Individual differences in second language learning*. London: Edward Arnold.

Yule, G., Hoffman, P., & Damico, J.(1987). Paying attention to pronunciation:The role of self-monitoring in perception. *TESOL Quarterly, 21*, 765–768.

Yule, G., Wetzel, S., & Kennedy, L. (1991). Listening perception accuracy of ESL learners as a variable function of speaker L1. *TESOL Quarterly, 24*, 219–223.

Also available from TESOL

All Things to All People
Donald C. Flemming, Lucie C. Germer, and Christiane Kelley

A New Decade of Language Testing Research:
Selected Papers From the 1990 Language Testing Research Colloquium
Dan Douglas and Carol Chapelle, Editors

Books for a Small Planet:
An Intercultural Bibliography for Young English Language Learners
Dorothy S. Brown

Common Threads of Practice:
Teaching English to Children Around the World
Katharine Davies Samway and Denise McKeon, Editors

Dialogue Journal Writing with Nonnative English Speakers:
A Handbook for Teachers
Joy Kreeft Peyton and Leslee Reed

Dialogue Journal Writing with Nonnative English Speakers:
An Instructional Packet for Teachers and Workshop Leaders
Joy Kreeft Peyton and Jana Staton

Discourse and Performance of International Teaching Assistants
Carolyn G. Madden and Cynthia L. Myers, Editors

Diversity as Resource:
Redefining Cultural Literacy
Denise E. Murray, Editor

New Ways in Teacher Education
Donald Freeman, with Steve Cornwell, Editors

New Ways in Teaching Reading
Richard R. Day, Editor

New Ways in Teaching Speaking
Kathleen M. Bailey and Lance Savage, Editors

Students and Teachers Writing Together:
Perspectives on Journal Writing
Joy Kreeft Peyton, Editor

Video in Second Language Teaching:
Using, Selecting, and Producing Video for the Classroom
Susan Stempleski and Paul Arcario, Editors

For more information, contact
Teachers of English to Speakers of Other Languages, Inc.
1600 Cameron Street, Suite 300
Alexandria, Virginia 22314 USA
Tel 703-836-0774 • Fax 703-836-7864